I0701960

GIANNI VALENTE

Beyond Fashion: The Path to Becoming a Personal Shopper and Image Consultant

GIANNI VALENTE

DEDICATION

To all those who see the world not only as it appears but as it could be.

To you, who find beauty and possibilities in every fold of fabric and every shade of color.

To those who dare to dream big, passionately pursuing their vision of elegance and style.

This book is dedicated to you: artists of image, sculptors of the possible, architects of the personal and the marvelous.

May every page inspire you to create, to explore, and to transform the world, one garment at a time.

CONTENTS

INTRODUCTION

Dear readers,

Welcome to an exploratory journey into the fascinating world of personal shopping and image consultancy, where elegance meets psychology, and art merges with communication. In these pages, you will unveil a universe where every style choice tells a story, every garment is a canvas, and every accessory is a brush that outlines a unique and irreplaceable identity.

This book is born from my passion for fashion and my years of experience as an image consultant. It is written for you, who are captivated by the transformative power of style and wish to discover how fashion can be a tool for personal and professional expression. It's for anyone looking to turn their passion for fashion into a rewarding career and for those seeking to deepen their understanding of personal image.

Fashion is a universal language, an art form that allows us to express who we are without the need for words. As an image consultant and personal shopper, I have learned that clothing is not just a matter of trends or brands; it's an ongoing dialogue with ourselves and the world around us. In this book, I will share my knowledge, experiences, and insights to guide you through the dynamic and creative world of personal shopping and image consultancy.

We will begin by exploring the importance of personal image in contemporary society and how it can influence not only others' perception but also our self-esteem and personal and professional success. I will show you how a carefully curated image can open doors and create opportunities, while a neglected image can close them.

After laying the foundations, we will delve into the heart of the personal shopper and image consultant profession. You will discover how to assess clients' needs and desires, create outfits that express their unique personality, and use clothing to communicate effectively without words. I will take you behind the scenes of the fashion world, showing you how to anticipate and interpret trends, select the right pieces for each client, and build a wardrobe that is both functional and representative.

This book is also a journey into the art of communication and the psychology of fashion. I will teach you to understand the silent language of colors and fabrics and how they can be used to enhance every type of figure and personality. Together, we will explore how clothing and accessories can be used to convey specific messages and how a well-crafted image can positively influence a person's life.

In the following chapters, we will delve into the practical techniques of the profession. I will guide you through the wardrobe analysis process, showing you how to identify what to keep, what to modify, and what to add. We will discuss the challenges and rewards of working with clients from different backgrounds and needs, and I will provide you with tools and tips for effectively managing client relationships.

Finally, this book will conclude with an overview of how to create and develop a successful career in the field of personal shopping and image consultancy. I will share my personal advice on building a strong reputation, acquiring clients, and maintaining consistent professional growth in this dynamic and ever-evolving industry.

This book is the result of years of experience, study, and observation. It is written with the aim to inspire, educate, and guide. I hope it offers you not only a deeper understanding of the world of personal shopping and image consultancy but also the tools to express your unique vision of style.

With this book, I invite you to embark on a journey of discovery and transformation, where fashion becomes a means to explore and celebrate the beauty of human diversity. Welcome to this extraordinary journey, where every step is an opportunity to create, innovate, and shine.

SHORT DESCRIPTION OF THE ROLES OF A PERSONAL SHOPPER AND IMAGE CONSULTANT

In the contemporary landscape of image and style, the personal shopper and image consultant emerge as highly important professional figures, being the creators and custodians of personal expression through fashion. These roles, infused with creativity, empathy, and technical expertise, play a crucial role in how individuals and professionals present themselves to the world.

The Personal Shopper: A personal shopper is much more than a mere shopping assistant; they are true navigators in the sea of fashion, experts who help untangle the complex webs of trends and adapt them to the unique needs of each client. This profession goes far beyond the mere selection of clothing and accessories; it entails a profound understanding of the client's personal, professional, and social needs. The personal shopper must possess encyclopedic knowledge of fashion, a keen intuition for the client's tastes and preferences, and the ability to anticipate unexpressed needs. They must be able to build a wardrobe that not only reflects the client's personal style but also enhances it on every occasion, from daily wear to special events. This professional figure is responsible for creating a tailor-made shopping experience, often balancing budget, personal style, and functionality, ensuring that every purchase is an investment in the client's well-being and image.

The Image Consultant: The image consultant takes care of the overall image and development of the client. This role requires a wide range of skills, from clothing consulting to managing aspects such as grooming, makeup, and even body language and etiquette. Working closely with clients, the image consultant must be able to listen to and interpret their desires and goals, translating them into a coherent and captivating image. An image consultant is often called upon to work in times of transition or personal renewal, such as career changes, significant life events, or simple desires for a fresh start. The approach requires sensitivity, discretion, and a careful evaluation of the client's physical characteristics, personality, and lifestyle. The process may include color analysis to determine the most flattering shades, figure assessment to select the most suitable cuts and styles, and the construction of a wardrobe that elevates the client's confidence and image.

In this book, we will delve into the heart of these professions, exploring in detail the skills, strategies, and challenges that personal shoppers and image consultants face daily. I will share personal experiences, practical advice, and lessons learned over the years, providing a comprehensive and in-depth insight into what it truly means to work in the field of image and personal style. Through these pages, you will discover how these professions can not only transform a person's wardrobe but also positively influence their self-esteem, professional success, and personal life.

THE IMPORTANCE OF THIS PROFESSION IN THE CONTEMPORARY WORLD

In an era characterized by a constant flow of information and an increasing focus on personal image, the profession of personal shopper and image consultant plays an increasingly significant role in the social and professional fabric. These style experts are not just fashion curators but essential interpreters of a rapidly evolving society, where personal image can significantly influence life opportunities, interpersonal relationships, and self-perception.

Professional and Social Impact:

We live in an age where the first impression plays a crucial role, often determining the course of our professional and social interactions. In an increasingly visual and interconnected world, clothing and personal image take on an even deeper meaning, influencing not only how others perceive us but also how we perceive ourselves. This dynamic is particularly evident in the professional sphere, where outward appearance can have a direct impact on career opportunities, working relationships, and communicative effectiveness.

In the Professional Context:

In a work environment, clothing is not just an ornament but a key element of non-verbal communication. It can convey messages of competence, reliability, and professionalism, or conversely, negligence or inadequacy. Decisions regarding hiring, promotions, and networking can be influenced, consciously or unconsciously, by the image we project. In this context, personal shoppers and image consultants become essential figures in helping professionals cultivate an image that matches their skills and ambitions. Appropriate clothing and personalized style can open doors in the world of work, facilitating positive interactions with colleagues, superiors, and clients. The right clothing can serve as a powerful tool for empowerment, giving the professional greater self-confidence, which in turn translates into a more assertive and influential presence.

Beyond Aesthetics:

The role of personal shoppers and image consultants goes far beyond selecting fashionable clothes. These professionals work to deeply understand the identity and professional goals of their clients, creating a look that not only reflects but also enhances their personal image. This is a careful strategy that takes into account the industry, corporate culture, and individual aspirations, aiming to build a consistent and authentic image. However, this process is not just a matter of aesthetics; it also concerns self-esteem and self-perception. A curated image and a wardrobe that reflects the true self can significantly boost self-confidence. When a person feels comfortable and confident in their clothing, this feeling also translates into how they move, speak, and interact with others.

Language of Image:

In a world where images often speak louder than words, personal shoppers and image consultants equip their clients with the tools needed to express themselves effectively and authentically. These professionals' ability to create a personal image that is in sync with the client's identity and aspirations is more than mere fashion advice; it is a form of strategic communication that can open new opportunities and improve the quality of professional and social relationships.

In summary, the role of personal shopper and image consultant in the contemporary context is indispensable for successfully navigating the professional world. These experts not only help build an attractive outward image but also contribute to shaping a strong sense of identity and confidence, key elements for success in all aspects of life.

Evolution of Fashion and Consumer Culture:

The advent of the digital age, with its ubiquitous social media and readily accessible e-commerce platforms, has radically transformed the fashion landscape. Never before have fashion trends and products been so accessible to a global audience. This democratization of fashion has brought undeniable benefits, making style and personal expression more free and diverse. However, it has also introduced unprecedented complexity into how consumers interact with fashion. In a world where new collections are launched every day, where every influencer showcases the latest "must-haves," and where advertising campaigns aim to capture our attention 24/7, choosing what to wear and what to buy can become an overwhelming experience. In this tumultuous context, the role of personal shoppers and image consultants takes on new and crucial importance.

Navigating the Overabundance of Options:

Personal shoppers and image consultants serve as expert guides in this sea of possibilities, helping clients navigate the countless options. It's not just about blindly following the latest trends but making thoughtful choices that reflect each individual's unique style. These professionals are tasked with filtering out the background noise of the fashion world, selecting pieces that are not only aesthetically pleasing but also reflect the character, values, and way of life of their clients.

Personalization and Values:

In an era marked by increasing awareness of ethical fashion, sustainability, and individuality, consumers are increasingly seeking to align their purchases with their personal values. Personal shoppers and image consultants thus become essential partners in the selection process, helping clients choose brands and products that not only enhance their outward appearance but also reflect their commitment to the environment, social responsibility, or ethical production.

A Holistic Approach to Fashion:

These experts offer a holistic approach to clothing and style, considering fashion not only as a set of trends but as an integrated aspect of the client's lifestyle. This includes understanding how garments fit into daily routines, the work context, special occasions, and the overall vision that the client has of themselves. Their task is to create a wardrobe that is not only aesthetically consistent but also functional and adaptable to the various needs of an individual's life.

Sustainability and Awareness:

Furthermore, personal shoppers and image consultants play a fundamental role in educating clients about sustainability and responsible fashion. They guide clients toward choices that are not only fashionable but also promote more conscious and environmentally friendly consumption. This may include selecting clothing made from sustainable materials, supporting small designers who adopt ethical practices, or encouraging the purchase of second-hand or vintage clothing.

In conclusion, in a world where fashion is ubiquitous and ever-evolving, personal shoppers and image consultants are actively contributing to shaping a more inclusive and diverse future of fashion. Their work goes beyond guiding clients in their style choices; it extends to promoting a more thoughtful and sustainable approach to fashion consumption. They help clients navigate a world overloaded with options, striking a balance between personal expression, ethical values, and practicality.

Psychological Well-being and Personal Image:

Clothing, often considered simply a social requirement or ornament, has a deep and complex connection with our psychological well-being and personal identity. Every style choice is a reflection of our personality, values, aspirations, and, in some cases, insecurities. In this intricate interplay between aesthetics and psyche, image consultants and personal shoppers emerge as key figures capable of understanding and harmonizing the client's external image with their internal identity, promoting a sense of well-being and authenticity.

Beyond Aesthetics:

These professionals go far beyond the simple choice of clothes that "look good." They work closely with clients to discover and enhance their true essence through clothing. It is a delicate and thoughtful process in which personal preferences, body type, skin color, profession, and even life goals play a fundamental role. An image consultant or personal shopper knows that a wardrobe change can be transformative, not only externally but also in terms of self-esteem and self-acceptance.

Impact on Mental Health:

In a world where personal image is often in the spotlight, the pressure to conform to certain aesthetic standards can be overwhelming. This can lead to issues of self-esteem and body image. An image consultant or personal shopper helps counter these issues, facilitating a healthier and more positive relationship with one's body and style. By teaching clients how to dress to highlight their strengths and to lovingly accept the parts of themselves they may perceive as flaws, these professionals can have a profoundly positive impact on their clients' mental health.

Building Confidence:

A key aspect of their work is building and strengthening clients' self-confidence. When a person wears clothes that truly reflect who they are, they move through the world with greater confidence and determination. This aspect is particularly relevant in contexts such as job interviews, important dates, or social events, where a curated image can open the door to new opportunities and connections.

Personalization and Empowerment:

The image consultant and personal shopper act as catalysts in the process of personal empowerment. They help clients express their individuality, encouraging style choices that do not blindly follow trends but reflect their unique personality. This process of personalizing clothing is an act of self-expression that can strengthen personal identity and promote greater self-awareness.

Reconnection with the Self:

Ultimately, the work of these professionals is a form of reconnection with the self. They help clients rediscover parts of themselves that may have been neglected or suppressed by external norms and expectations. Through their guidance, clients learn to see clothing not only as a necessity or duty but as a means to celebrate their individuality and navigate the world with a renewed sense of authenticity and confidence. The role of an image consultant or personal shopper is, in short, essential in today's image-focused society. They not only guide fashion choices but also help people strike a balance between aesthetics and inner well-being, proving essential for mental health and self-esteem in a world that increasingly values personal image.

Inclusivity and Diversity:

In an era where diversity and inclusivity are becoming increasingly integral to our social fabric, the role of the personal shopper and image consultant takes on an even deeper and more significant dimension. These professionals, interacting daily with a wide range of clients from different cultural backgrounds, ethnicities, ages, genders, and body shapes, are at the forefront of promoting an approach to fashion that not only respects but actively celebrates the richness of human diversity.

Beyond Traditional Fashion Barriers:

Traditionally, the fashion industry has often been criticized for its tendency to promote a singular and unrepresentative beauty ideal. Today, personal shoppers and image consultants are actively challenging these outdated stereotypes, working to create a space where every individual can feel seen, heard, and valued. This involves going beyond traditional beauty standards to embrace and celebrate beauty in all its forms and manifestations.

Personalization and Acceptance:

These professionals adopt a personalized approach that takes into account the specific needs of each client, ensuring that everyone can find their own style that reflects their unique identity. This process of personalization is crucial not only for the comfort and satisfaction of the client but also for promoting a broader message of acceptance and inclusivity. By helping clients feel comfortable and confident in their style, they contribute to building a society where diversity is not only accepted but celebrated.

Contribution to Fashion Culture:

In this context, personal shoppers and image consultants assume the role of cultural influencers, contributing to shaping a more inclusive and diverse fashion culture. Their ability to listen and respond to the needs of a broad spectrum of clients makes them key actors in promoting positive change in the fashion industry. They serve as a bridge between consumers and fashion creators, providing feedback that can guide future trends toward greater inclusivity.

Challenging Stereotypes:

Working with clients of all ages, sizes, shapes, and cultural backgrounds, these style experts help challenge prevailing stereotypes and enrich the discourse on fashion and personal image. They demonstrate that style and elegance have no barriers and that fashion can be a powerful means of expression for everyone. Through their work, they help spread a message of tolerance and openness, showing that beauty and style know no bounds.

A More Inclusive Future:

Ultimately, personal shoppers and image consultants are actively contributing to building a more inclusive and representative future of fashion. Their work is not limited to guiding clients in their style choices; it extends to promoting a more thoughtful and accepting approach to fashion. They help shape a world in which every person can feel valued and respected, regardless of their shape, size, or background.

Adaptability and Innovation:

In an ever-evolving industry like fashion, personal shoppers and image consultants must constantly update themselves and be ready to adapt. This profession requires not only a deep knowledge of current trends but also the ability to anticipate changes in the industry, adapting to new technologies and changing customer expectations.

In conclusion, in an era where image has become a global language, personal shoppers and image consultants play a guiding and inspiring role, helping people navigate the complex world of fashion with confidence and awareness. Their work is not just a matter of style but a fundamental act of communication and personal expression, a key element for success and well-being in the modern era.

THE IMPORTANCE OF IMAGE

Inglese: "The Importance of Image in an era dominated by visual immediacy and digital communication, personal image assumes a primary role in contemporary society. This is not simply a matter of vanity or superficial aesthetics; rather, image has become a powerful tool of communication, a silent language that speaks before words are even uttered.

Non-Verbal Communication

Non-verbal communication, a fundamental component of how we interact with the world, extends far beyond gestures or facial expressions; it is intricately intertwined with the choices we make every day regarding our appearance. The clothes we choose to wear, how we groom ourselves, and even our posture and body language are all elements that contribute to our non-verbal communication, profoundly influencing how others perceive us and, ultimately, the quality of our social and professional interactions.

Silent Signals: The clothes we wear function as a silent code, conveying messages to others about our social status, personality, values, and even our mood and intentions. This visual language goes beyond fleeting fashion trends; it reflects our identity and how we relate to the world. In professional contexts, well-groomed attire can communicate professionalism and reliability, while in social settings, it can express openness, creativity, or other personality traits.

Impact on Interactions and Opportunities: Non-verbal communication through clothing and personal image plays a key role in our daily interactions. It can influence the first impression we make, the trust and respect we earn from others, and even the opportunities presented to us in both our professional and personal lives. A well-crafted image can open doors and create an immediate connection, while a neglected or mismatched image can lead to misunderstandings or negative evaluations.

Reflection of Personality and Mood: Our clothing choices often serve as an external reflection of our internal state. Clothing that makes us feel comfortable and confident can significantly boost our self-esteem and positively affect our behavior and body language. Conversely, clothing in which we feel uncomfortable or out of place can have the opposite effect, negatively impacting our posture and self-assurance.

Culture, Context, and Perception: Non-verbal communication through clothing is also deeply influenced by cultural and social context. What is considered appropriate or attractive in one culture may not be in another. This cultural awareness is essential, especially in a globalized world where interactions often occur between individuals from diverse cultural backgrounds. A sensitive understanding of these differences can enhance communication and foster positive interpersonal relationships.

Role of Image Professionals: Faced with these challenges, image professionals such as personal shoppers and image consultants play a crucial role. They help their clients navigate the complex world of non-verbal communication by selecting clothing and accessories that not only make them feel comfortable and confident but also effectively communicate their intentions, status, and personality. Through their expert guidance, clients can learn how to use clothing and personal image to express the best version of themselves, both in professional and personal contexts.

In conclusion, non-verbal communication through personal image is a fundamental element of our daily interaction with the world. A well-crafted and conscious image can open multiple doors and create positive connections, enhancing our self-perception and how others perceive us.

Psychological Impact

In addition to influencing others' perceptions, image also has a profound psychological impact on the individual who wears it. How we dress and present ourselves can directly influence our self-esteem and self-confidence. A well-groomed image can instill a sense of control and competence, while a neglected image can have the opposite effect. This phenomenon, known as "enclothed cognition," underscores how clothing can alter not only others' perception of us but also our self-perception.

Psychological Impact of Personal Image: Personal image, particularly how we dress, has a deep and often underestimated impact on our psychological well-being. This relationship between clothing and psyche, known as "enclothed cognition," goes beyond the superficial, significantly influencing how we feel about ourselves and the world around us.

Enclothed Cognition: "Enclothed cognition" refers to the phenomenon where the characteristics of the clothing we wear can influence our behavior, attitudes, and how we process information. This concept goes beyond the idea that "dressing for success" can influence others' impressions; it suggests that what we wear can change our own sense of competence and reliability. For example, wearing formal attire can not only enhance others' perception of our professionalism but can also increase our own feeling of competence and trustworthiness.

Self-Esteem and Body Image: How we manage our personal image is strongly correlated with our self-esteem and body image. Dressing in a way that we feel reflects our true identity can boost self-confidence and promote greater acceptance of our bodies. Conversely, wearing clothing in which we do not feel comfortable can exacerbate body dissatisfaction and diminish self-esteem.

Effect on Behavior and Emotions: Clothing can also influence our behavior and emotions. Wearing something we love and feel comfortable in can improve our mood and overall disposition. This can lead to improved interpersonal relationships, productivity, and even creativity. Furthermore, the act of consciously choosing clothing can be a mindfulness exercise, helping us connect with the present moment and ourselves.

Personalization and Self-Expression: The process of selecting clothing is also a powerful means of personal expression. Having control over how we present ourselves to the world can be an act of self-expression and a way to communicate aspects of our personality without words. This form of personal expression is particularly important during periods of change or transition, where new clothing styles can reflect internal evolutions or desires for renewal.

Role of Image Professionals: In this context, the work of personal shoppers and image consultants becomes a powerful tool for enhancing psychological well-being. By guiding their clients in choosing clothing that not only makes them look their best but also reflects their personality and aspirations, these professionals can have a tangible impact on how clients see and feel about themselves. Through a well-crafted and personalized image, they contribute to building greater self-confidence and a sense of authenticity in their clients.

In summary, personal image and clothing choices have a significant impact not only on how others perceive us but also on our psychological well-being. Conscious image management can be a powerful tool for self-esteem, empowerment, and self-expression.

Image in the Professional Context

Image in the workplace is a fundamental aspect that goes beyond mere aesthetic appearance. In an increasingly competitive and visually-oriented professional world, the image we project can have a direct and significant impact on our careers. This concept is particularly relevant in an era where the first impression is often formed even before a face-to-face meeting, thanks to the prevalence of social media and online professional platforms.

Impact on Professional Perception: A professional and appropriate appearance is a key factor in communicating competence, reliability, and seriousness. In many sectors, clothing and personal image are seen as extensions of an individual's professionalism. A well-groomed appearance that aligns with industry expectations can pave the way for new opportunities, facilitate relationships with clients and colleagues, and enhance the perception of credibility and authority. Conversely, a neglected or inappropriate image can lead to negative judgments, diminish the perception of professional competence, and limit career advancement opportunities.

Role in Personal Branding: In an era where personal branding has become crucial, personal image is often considered a key element of personal branding. Clothing, personal grooming, and body language are components that contribute to defining our professional identity. A consistent and well-crafted image can strengthen our personal brand, helping us stand out in a crowded job market and build a respected and solid reputation.

Sectoral and Cultural Differences: It is important to recognize that norms related to professional image can vary significantly depending on the industry and cultural context. What is considered appropriate in a creative environment may not be in a more conservative corporate setting. Awareness of these differences is essential for successfully navigating the professional world and effectively interacting with colleagues and clients from diverse backgrounds.

Impact on Working Relationships: An appropriate professional image can also facilitate the creation of positive work relationships. It can help establish a relationship of trust and respect with colleagues and clients, creating a more harmonious and productive work environment. Additionally, a professional appearance can positively influence our self-perception in the workplace, increasing self-confidence and improving our performance.

Professional Image Consultation: In this context, the role of an image consultant or personal shopper becomes significantly valuable. They can offer expert guidance on how to present oneself optimally in a professional setting, taking into account the specific requirements of the industry and the client's personal preferences. The goal is to create an image that is not only aesthetically pleasing but also effectively communicates the client's professional qualities and personal value.

In conclusion, image in the professional context is a crucial aspect that should be carefully nurtured with attention and awareness. A strategic management of one's image can open new professional doors, strengthen personal branding, and enhance working relationships, emphasizing the importance of considering clothing and personal grooming not only as a matter of style but as integral components of professional success.

Diversity and Inclusion

In a world characterized by a growing recognition of diversity and the need for inclusivity, personal image assumes a fundamental role as a vehicle for expression and celebration of individual uniqueness. This approach to image goes beyond mere aesthetics, becoming a powerful tool for promoting respect and appreciation for cultural, gender, age, and all other forms of human diversity.

Celebration of Individual Uniqueness: In a global context where cultures intertwine and identities are more fluid, image becomes a means to express and celebrate this rich variety of human experiences. Dressing in a way that reflects one's culture, gender identity, age, or any other personal characteristic is an act of self-affirmation and pride. Image professionals have the task of helping their clients find a style that not only makes them feel valued and comfortable but also authentically represents who they are.

Challenging Stereotypes: Through image, it is possible to challenge stereotypes and prejudices that often surround certain identities or cultural groups. A well-groomed and conscious image can contribute to dismantling biases and promoting a more open and inclusive view of society. In particular, in professional contexts, an inclusive image can help create more welcoming and respectful work environments, where diversity is seen as an asset rather than an obstacle.

Respect for Cultural Differences: In a globalized world, respecting and understanding diverse cultural norms related to clothing and personal image is crucial. What is considered appropriate or fashionable in one culture may have very different meanings in another. Image consultants and personal shoppers, therefore, must have a deep and sensitive understanding of these differences to guide their clients in choices that are respectful and appropriate.

Gender and Age Inclusivity: In the realm of fashion and image, inclusivity also pertains to the representation and appreciation of all ages and gender identities. Creating styles that respect and celebrate gender diversity and the evolution of style throughout a person's life is a crucial aspect of the work of image professionals.

This involves going beyond traditional standards and stereotypes related to age and gender, embracing a more flexible and personalized view of style.

Promotion of Constructive Dialogue: Personal image can also serve as a starting point for broader conversations about diversity and inclusivity. Through conscious and respectful choices of clothing and accessories, image professionals and their clients can contribute to promoting constructive dialogue on these important issues, fostering understanding and acceptance of differences.

In an era that increasingly values diversity and inclusivity, personal image becomes a powerful tool for expression, respect, and celebration of the uniqueness of each individual. Image consultants and personal shoppers play a crucial role in guiding their clients toward style choices that not only reflect who they are but also contribute to building a more open and inclusive society.

Role of Image Professionals

In the increasingly complex and multifaceted ecosystem of fashion and personal style, image professionals such as personal shoppers and image consultants play a vital role. Their expertise goes far beyond simply selecting clothing; they are true interpreters and navigators of the world of image, assisting clients in charting a personal and meaningful path through the endless possibilities of fashion.

Harmonizing Image with Internal Identity: One of the fundamental aspects of their work is harmonizing the client's external image with their internal identity. Image professionals help clients express who they truly are through their clothing, ensuring that the external image faithfully reflects the client's personality, values, and life goals. This process goes beyond selecting clothing that "looks good" and focuses on creating a style that speaks of the individual, their history, and their aspirations.

Guiding Toward Authentic Self-Expression: Personal shoppers and image consultants act as guides in the journey toward authentic self-expression. They work to deeply understand the client – their tastes, needs, and lifestyle – and translate this information into style choices that enhance their uniqueness. This process may include discovering new styles, exploring colors and fabrics that best express the client's personality, or refreshing a wardrobe to mark a new phase in life.

Improving Quality of Life and Self-Esteem: Their role goes beyond aesthetics; it has a direct impact on clients' quality of life and self-esteem. Dressing in a way that makes us feel authentic and comfortable can significantly boost self-confidence and overall well-being. Image professionals, through their skills and sensitivity, help clients achieve this level of comfort and confidence, positively influencing both their personal and professional lives.

Adaptability and Cultural Competence: In a globalized and culturally diverse world, image professionals must possess strong adaptability and cultural competence. They must be able to navigate and respect a variety of cultural norms, styles, and expectations, offering guidance that is sensitive and inclusive. This adaptability is essential not only to meet the diverse needs of clients but also to contribute to a more open and diverse fashion landscape.

Innovation and Trends: In addition to guiding clients in their personal style choices, image professionals must also stay updated with the latest trends and innovations in the world of fashion. This doesn't mean blindly following every new trend but rather understanding current trends and integrating them intelligently and personalized into clients' style choices, ensuring they remain contemporary while staying true to their personal style.

In conclusion, image professionals play a fundamental role in the contemporary world of fashion and style. Their ability to translate the complexity of personal identity and fashion into a coherent and authentic image is an essential component in the process of self-expression and self-realization for an individual.

In summary, personal image is much more than a mere aesthetic aspect; it is an essential form of communication, a means of self-expression, and a crucial factor for personal success and well-being. Therefore, image care is not just a matter of fashion but a vital skill for effectively navigating in an increasingly visual and interconnected society.

IMPACT OF PERSONAL IMAGE ON PERCEPTION AND SELF-ESTEEM

Personal Image is a fundamental component of an individual's identity and plays a critical role in both how others perceive us and our self-esteem. This bidirectional relationship between how we see ourselves and how we are seen by others is deeply intertwined with our outward image, which includes clothing, grooming, body language, and overall expression.

Perception by Others

Personal image, in all its forms, serves as a powerful channel of non-verbal communication that precedes and accompanies our interactions. Before a word is even exchanged, our outward appearance sends a series of signals and messages that others interpret, consciously or unconsciously, to form an opinion about us.

Visual Narrative: Every element of our appearance, from the clothes we wear to how we style our hair, from our posture to our movement, contributes to building a visual narrative about who we are. This narrative tells stories about our background, current mood, personal tastes and preferences, and even our aspirations. In formal contexts, such as the workplace, a professional and well-groomed presentation can communicate seriousness, reliability, and competence. In more casual settings, personal image can reflect our relaxed personality or our hobbies and interests.

Impact on First Impressions: First impressions are often lasting and challenging to alter. The image we project in the initial stages of an encounter can determine the direction of future interactions. If we present a well-groomed and context-appropriate image, we are more likely to be perceived as reliable, competent, and pleasant to be around. This aspect is particularly relevant in situations like job interviews, business meetings, or significant social events.

Consistency between Image and Identity: Consistency between our outward image and our internal identity is essential for conveying authenticity. A significant discrepancy between how we present ourselves and who we truly are can lead to misunderstandings or misconceptions about us. When the outward image is in harmony with the internal identity, it communicates a sense of authenticity and confidence that is attractive and reassuring to others.

Consequences of a Neglected Image: On the contrary, a neglected or inconsistent image can lead to being perceived as less professional, less reliable, or less competent. In some cases, it can also negatively impact our credibility and the trust others place in us. This aspect can be particularly problematic in professional environments, where personal image may be seen as a reflection of professionalism and attention to detail.

Role of Image Professionals: Image professionals, understanding the importance of these aspects, work to help their clients develop an image that is not only aesthetically pleasing but also effectively communicates who they are and what they represent. They provide guidance not only on what to wear but also on how to carry themselves so that their outward image is an authentic reflection of their personality and lifestyle.

Personal image is a fundamental aspect of non-verbal communication. Consciously managing one's image can have a significant impact on how others perceive and interact with us, thus decisively influencing our social and professional opportunities.

Self-Esteem and Self-Efficacy

Depth of Psychological Impact of Clothing: Beyond mere "enclothed cognition," there are multiple psychological layers defining the relationship between our clothing and self-perception. For instance, choosing clothes that we believe express our true identity can serve as a powerful tool for self-affirmation. This act of self-expression, when aligned with our values and aspirations, can bolster our self-esteem and confidence in our abilities.

Impact of Fit and Comfort: The comfort and fit of clothing are crucial factors influencing our self-efficacy. Well-fitted and comfortable attire can enhance the sense of competence and control. This aspect is particularly relevant in high-pressure situations, such as job interviews or public presentations, where self-confidence is essential.

Clothing as Psychological Armor: For many people, clothing can function as a kind of "psychological armor," providing a sense of security and protection in challenging social situations. Wearing an outfit in which one feels particularly comfortable or powerful can be a way to cope with social anxiety or increase the feeling of control in a challenging environment.

Relationship between Fashion and Personal Identity: Fashion is not only a tool to impress others but also a means to explore and assert our own identity. The ability to experiment and play with different styles can be a path to greater self-understanding and self-acceptance. This process of exploration and assertion through fashion can lead to increased self-esteem and self-efficacy.

The Role of Image Professionals in Empowerment: Image professionals, such as personal shoppers and image consultants, can play a crucial role in empowering their clients through fashion. They can help clients discover styles that enhance not only their appearance but also their self-perception. This process goes beyond choosing aesthetically pleasing clothing and focuses on finding garments that truly resonate with the individual, thus enhancing their self-esteem and self-efficacy.

We can affirm that personal image and clothing are intimately connected to our self-esteem and self-efficacy. Fashion provides a unique means to express and reinforce our identity, improve our self-perception, and navigate social and professional interactions with greater confidence.

Group Dynamics and Belonging

Personal image has a significant influence on group dynamics and belonging, both in social and professional contexts. This dynamic extends far beyond simply adhering to a dress code; it reflects an understanding and adherence to certain cultural and social norms that are essential for integration and acceptance within a group.

Expression of Group Values: How we dress can be a powerful statement of alignment with the values and norms of a particular group. For example, in a corporate environment, adhering to the dress code can communicate respect for corporate conventions and a desire to fit in. In social contexts, clothing can reflect membership in certain cultural or social groups, expressing solidarity or shared specific values or interests.

Navigating Different Contexts: The ability to adapt one's image based on the context requires a careful understanding of the expectations and norms of each environment. This requires a sort of social fluidity and flexibility, where a person can alter their style to reflect the environment they are in while maintaining a sense of personal authenticity. This ability to navigate different contexts is a valuable social skill that facilitates communication and integration.

Managing Otherness: In situations where an individual

deliberately deviates from the clothing norms of a group, a perception of "otherness" can be created. While in some cases, this may be an act of self-expression and affirmation of a unique identity, in others, it can lead to challenges in terms of integration and acceptance within the group. It is important to recognize when and how to express one's individuality through clothing, balancing personal expression with respect for the group's norms.

Role in Strengthening Group Identity: Sharing a common style of dress within a group can also work to strengthen collective identity and a sense of belonging. This can be seen in professional groups, cultural communities, sports teams, and other social contexts where a certain type of clothing or accessory becomes a symbol of unity and belonging.

Implications for Diversity and Inclusivity: In contexts that value diversity and inclusivity, it is important to consider how image and clothing norms can be inclusive and respectful of individual differences. Creating environments where people feel free to express their identity through clothing while respecting the general group norms is essential to promoting a sense of acceptance and belonging.

In summary, personal image and clothing choice play a fundamental role in group dynamics and belonging. The ability to adapt one's image appropriately to various social and professional contexts while maintaining a sense of personal authenticity is a key social skill that influences our ability to integrate and interact effectively with others.

Managing Personal Image

Conscious management of personal image is a key element for success and well-being in all areas of life. In the era of visual communication and social media, the ability to present an image that is both authentic and contextually appropriate can have a significant impact on others' perceptions, professional opportunities, and interpersonal relationships.

Authenticity and Adaptability: At the heart of managing personal image is finding a balance between authenticity and adaptability. On one hand, it is crucial that the image we project reflects our true identity, values, and personality. This not only boosts our self-esteem but also the confidence others place in us. On the other hand, being able to adapt our image to the diverse needs of the social and professional contexts we find ourselves in is equally important to ensure our acceptance and success in those environments.

Strategies for Managing Personal Image: Effective personal image management requires a series of conscious strategies. This includes understanding non-verbal language and the meaning behind various style choices, as well as awareness of how certain styles, colors, or clothing can be interpreted in different contexts. It also implies the ability for self-analysis and adaptation, continuously evaluating how our image choices align with our personal and professional goals.

Importance of Context: Every social or professional context has its own norms and expectations regarding image. Understanding these norms and adapting our personal image accordingly is crucial to facilitate interactions and to be positively perceived. This can vary significantly across different professional sectors, social events, or even among different cultures.

Reflection and Personal Growth: Managing personal image is not a static process; it is a journey of continuous reflection and growth. As we evolve as individuals, our image should also evolve to reflect changes in our identity, lifestyle, and aspirations. This process of adaptation and growth contributes not only to our external success but also to our inner development.

Role of Image Professionals: For those seeking to optimize their personal image, image professionals such as personal shoppers and image consultants can offer invaluable guidance. They can help identify styles that best suit the client's personality and goals, as well as provide advice on how to navigate the complexities of various social and professional contexts.

As you can understand, effective personal image management is a fundamental skill in the modern era. Being able to present an image that is both authentic and contextually appropriate can make the difference between achieving success and not realizing one's full potential. It is a dynamic balance that requires awareness, adaptability, and ongoing self-exploration.

In conclusion, personal image is much more than a superficial aspect; it is a key element of our identity and a crucial factor in defining our relationships with others and with ourselves. Thoughtful and conscious management of personal image can lead to increased self-esteem, professional success, and personal satisfaction.

RELEVANT STUDIES AND STATISTICS

Studies on 'Enclothed Cognition': These studies explore how the clothing we wear influences our behavior, attitudes, and even decision-making processes. Research in this field can provide data on how specific types of clothing can enhance self-confidence, performance in specific tasks, or the perception of authority and competence.

Research on the Impact of Clothing on Professional Success: Some studies focus on how clothing influences the perception of professionalism and reliability in the workplace. These may include statistics on how clothing affects the likelihood of being hired, promoted, or perceived as leaders.

Analysis of the Impact of Personal Image on First Impressions: There is research that investigates how quickly we form judgments based on outward appearance and how these judgments influence our interactions. These studies can offer interesting data on the duration of the impact of a first impression and which aspects of the image are most influential.

Research on Fashion and Social Identity: These studies explore how clothing and personal style are linked to social, cultural, and gender identity. They may include data on how different social groups use fashion to express their identity or belonging to a group.

Studies on Consumer Psychology in Fashion: These studies examine how consumers choose and purchase clothing, with a focus on aspects such as the influence of social media, sustainable consumption trends, or the impact of advertising and marketing in the fashion industry.

Impact of Clothing on Cognitive Performance: Some psychological studies have explored the concept of 'enclothed cognition,' demonstrating how clothing can influence cognitive performance and behavior. For example, wearing a lab coat has been linked to increased attention and accuracy in certain tasks, suggesting that clothing can affect how we process information and solve problems.

Relationship between Fashion and Self-esteem: Research in psychology has also examined how clothing choice is related to our self-esteem. Clothing can act as a form of self-expression that, if in line with our personal identity, can boost self-confidence and psychological well-being.

Influence of Fashion on Social Dynamics: Sociological studies have investigated how clothing influences social perception, stratification, and group dynamics. Clothing can serve as an indicator of social status, group membership, or even personal values, thus influencing social interactions and relationships.

Clothing and Professional Perception: In the professional context, numerous studies have examined the impact of clothing on perceptions of competence and credibility. A well-groomed and professional appearance can not only influence how others perceive us but also increase our perception of self-efficacy in the workplace.

Fashion Consumption and Sustainability: In the context of growing environmental and sustainability concerns, research has begun to focus on consumer behavior in the fashion industry. These studies explore themes such as conscious consumption, the environmental impact of fashion production, and consumer interest in sustainable fashion brands.

FREQUENTLY ASKED QUESTIONS: HOW DOES IMAGE INFLUENCE DAILY LIFE?

How does personal image influence social relationships?

Personal image plays a significant role in how we interact and are perceived in social settings. A well-groomed appearance that aligns with our identity can facilitate social interactions, boost self-confidence, and help us express our personality.

Can clothing really impact my self-esteem?

Yes, clothing has a direct impact on self-esteem. Dressing in a way that makes us feel comfortable and reflects our identity can significantly increase self-confidence and overall well-being.

Does my personal image affect my professional opportunities?

Absolutely. A professional and context-appropriate image can influence how colleagues and superiors perceive you, increasing opportunities for success and career advancement.

Is it important to adapt my style to the context?

Yes, adapting your style to the context is crucial. Wearing appropriate attire for the situation demonstrates respect and social awareness, and it can positively influence how others perceive you.

How can my personal image influence my love life?

Personal image is often the first aspect others notice in a romantic context. Presenting yourself in a way that reflects who you truly are can help attract people who appreciate your authentic personality, fostering more genuine and satisfying relationships.

Does personal image play a role in my mental health?

Yes, personal image can influence mental health. Dressing in a way that makes you feel confident and authentic can improve your mood and self-esteem, contributing to better overall mental health.

How can I balance fashion and comfort?

Balancing fashion and comfort involves finding a middle ground between what is stylish and what makes you feel comfortable. Experimenting with different styles and fabrics can help you discover what works best for you.

Can changing my style affect my self-perception?

Changing your style can have a significant impact on your self-perception. Experimenting with new looks can be a way to explore different facets of your personality and discover new aspects of yourself.

Is personal image important even when I work from home?

Yes, maintaining a well-groomed personal image even when working from home can positively influence your productivity and mood. Dressing in a way that makes you feel professional, even in a home environment, can help you maintain a clear distinction between work and personal time.

How can I develop my personal style?

Developing your personal style takes time and experimentation. Start by identifying what you like, what makes you feel comfortable, and what reflects your personality. Consider consulting an image consultant for personalized advice.

These frequently asked questions highlight the importance and breadth of the topic of personal image, demonstrating how it impacts various aspects of daily life.

DEBUNKED MYTHS: IMAGE ONLY MATTERS IN A PROFESSIONAL CONTEXT

Importance Beyond the Professional: The myth that image is relevant only in professional contexts ignores the significant role it plays in numerous other aspects of life. Personal image has a profound impact not only on professional success but also on social relationships, mental health, love life, and self-esteem.

Social Relationships and First Impressions: In social interactions, personal image is often the first thing noticed. This affects the first impression and can set the tone for future interactions. A well-groomed and authentic image can facilitate the creation of meaningful connections and improve the quality of social relationships.

Image and Mental Health: Our personal image can directly influence how we perceive ourselves and, consequently, our mental health. Dressing in a way that makes us feel confident and authentic can have a positive effect on our self-esteem and overall mood.

Love Life and Personal Attraction: In love life, personal image plays a fundamental role in attraction and romance. An appearance that reflects our true personality can help us attract partners who appreciate who we truly are, contributing to more satisfying and authentic relationships.

Self-Expression and Personal Identity: Personal image is a powerful tool for self-expression. Through our choices of clothing and style, we can express our identity, values, and uniqueness.

This aspect of image is crucial for our sense of identity and can influence our perception of who we are.

Effects on Productivity and Well-Being: Even in non-professional contexts, such as working from home or daily activities, personal image can influence productivity and well-being. Dressing in a way that makes us feel prepared and focused can increase efficiency and help us maintain a clear distinction between work and personal time.

Cultural and Social Impact: Personal image also has a cultural and social impact. It can be a way to express belonging to a cultural or social group or to participate in cultural movements or fashion trends that reflect social values or ideals.

Adaptability and Personal Growth: Finally, personal image is a dynamic aspect of our lives that evolves with us. The ability to adapt our image to reflect changes in our personal life and goals is an important part of personal growth and development.

In summary, personal image goes beyond the professional context. It is intrinsically linked to many aspects of our lives, influencing our interactions with others, our self-perception, and our place in the social and cultural world. Debunking the myth that image only matters professionally is essential to recognize and value its overall role in our daily lives.

THE IMAGE CONSULTANT

In the diverse realm of fashion and personal image, the image consultant emerges as a reference figure, an artist, and a confidant whose work goes far beyond mere clothing selection. This professional delves into the personal stories of their clients, listening, interpreting, and translating their dreams, aspirations, and needs into an image that authentically represents them.

The true art of an image consultant doesn't solely reside in their knowledge of fashion trends or their ability to pick the perfect outfit for an occasion. Instead, it lies in their skill to intuit and celebrate the unique personality of each client, understanding the nuances of their lifestyle, the intricacies of their character, the nature of their work, and even their insecurities and fears. It's a job that requires an empathetic touch, fine sensitivity, and deep listening ability.

In this journey of transformation and self-discovery, the image consultant addresses not only clothing. Every detail, from grooming to makeup, posture to gestures, is considered to create a harmonious and consistent image. The goal is to bring out the intrinsic beauty of each individual, reinforcing their confidence and self-esteem.

The image consultant thus becomes a coach, an ally in the client's personal growth journey. Sometimes, this role requires going beyond fashion, working on self-image and self-acceptance. In this sense, the image consultant has the power to profoundly influence people's lives, helping them see themselves in a new, brighter, and more authentic light.

Cultural sensitivity and adaptability are indispensable qualities in this profession. The image consultant must navigate different cultural norms, respecting the traditions and values of each client while skillfully guiding them towards an image that celebrates their uniqueness in every context.

Lastly, while following trends is part of the job, the best image consultants know when to deviate from the beaten path. They have an eye for recognizing and valuing what makes each person special and unique, regardless of current fashion trends. In them, clients find a personality artist, an image architect who builds bridges between internal essence and external expression.

Ultimately, an image consultant is much more than a fashion expert: they are a visual storyteller, an identity translator, and a catalyst for personal change. Through their guidance, people not only change how they dress but often how they see and feel about themselves in the world.

In the diverse and multifaceted world of personal image, the role of an image consultant is defined by a set of unique and multifunctional skills, intertwining knowledge of fashion, psychology, the art of communication, and interpersonal sensitivity.

Role of an Image Consultant: A Mosaic of Responsibilities

At its deepest essence, the role of an image consultant unfolds as a true art of personal interpretation. This professional figure goes beyond being a fashion trend expert or a selector of trendy clothing; instead, they configure themselves as true sculptors of visual identity, artisans of personality who work with the canvas of the wardrobe to capture and reflect the unique essence of each individual.

The mission of an image consultant goes far beyond creating a visually appealing look; their true art lies in the ability to grasp and interpret the complexity of the individual, to listen to their stories, passions, fears, and dreams. It's a process that delves deep, digging into the psychology of the client, their core values, and aspirations, and then weaving these elements into a visual image that is not only harmonious and cohesive but also faithfully reflects the individuality of the person.

In this process, the consultant operates as a detailed analyst of identity, dedicating time and energy to understand every facet of the client. It's an active listening that goes beyond words, capturing non-verbal signals, emotional expressions, and the silent language of the body. This deep understanding is what allows the consultant to make style choices that are not only aesthetically valid but also resonate with the client's soul.

The image consultant, therefore, is not just a master of fashion but also a visual storyteller who uses clothes and accessories as metaphors and symbols of the client's personal story. Every style choice, every combination of colors, every selected accessory becomes part of a larger narrative, a visual storytelling that celebrates the individual's uniqueness.

Furthermore, the image consultant acts as a bridge between the individual and the external world. Their skill lies in balancing the client's personal expression with the expectations and norms of the context in which they operate, be it professional, social, or personal. It's a delicate balance between authenticity and adaptability, requiring not only creativity and intuition but also a deep cultural and social awareness.

In conclusion, the role of an image consultant is a complex mosaic of responsibilities, requiring a wide range of skills and deep sensitivity. It goes beyond the surface, touching the deepest chords of human existence and reflecting the rich tapestry of personal identity through clothing and style.

Required Skills: A Symphony of Abilities

In-Depth Knowledge of Fashion: Naturally, a solid understanding of fashion, its trends, fabrics, cuts, and colors is fundamental. The consultant must stay updated on the latest trends but also have historical knowledge of fashion to draw from a vast repertoire of styles.

Listening and Empathy: Perhaps one of the most crucial skills is the ability to truly listen to clients. Understanding their desires, insecurities, and dreams is essential to create an image that authentically represents them.

Non-Verbal Communication Skills: The consultant must understand and use the non-verbal language of clothing. Every style choice communicates specific messages; the consultant must know how these messages can be interpreted in various social and professional contexts.

Psychological and Social Sensitivity: Understanding the psychological dynamics that influence self-perception and body image is essential. Additionally, sensitivity to various cultural and social norms ensures that style suggestions are respectful and appropriate.

Creativity and Artistic Vision: The image consultant must have an artistic eye, capable of visualizing and creating a look that is unique and personal, going beyond standardized models of beauty and style.

Flexibility and Adaptability: The ability to adapt to a wide range of clients with different needs and backgrounds is crucial. Each client requires a personalized approach that takes into account their individual specificities.

Technical Styling Skills: From the basics of color matching to knowledge of body proportions, the consultant must possess technical skills to effectively advise clients on style choices that enhance their figure.

In conclusion, the role of an image consultant is complex and multifaceted, requiring a range of skills that go beyond simply choosing clothing. It's a role that demands intuition, sensitivity, creativity, and a deep understanding of human nature, all aimed at enhancing individual uniqueness through personal image.

In this journey through the world of image consulting, we will explore some case studies and successful examples that illustrate the wide range of impacts this profession can have. These stories are the result of a fictional narrative but are based on realistic and plausible scenarios, offering a glimpse into the transformative potential of an image consultant.

Case Study 1: The Rebirth of a Professional

John, a middle-aged executive in a renowned consulting firm, found himself in a stagnant phase of his career. Despite his extensive experience and expertise, he felt that something was holding him back. His wardrobe, consisting of traditional gray and navy blue suits, reflected an outdated image of the corporate world, not in line with his entrepreneurial spirit and innovative mindset.

The turning point came when John decided to work with an image consultant. Initially skeptical, he soon realized that the change was not just about aesthetics but a deeper renewal of his personal image. The consultant, after listening to John's stories, aspirations, and professional goals, proposed a revolutionary approach. Together, they decided to introduce more modern and bold style elements into John's wardrobe while maintaining an air of professionalism.

They started by adding tailored blazers in vibrant colors like burgundy and teal, paired with custom-made shirts in subtly elegant shades. They ditched conventional ties in favor of contemporary accessories like silk scarves and artistic cufflinks. Even the shoes underwent an upgrade, transitioning from classic Oxfords to more modern models with intriguing details.

As his wardrobe transformed, John's attitude also underwent a change. He began to feel more confident, and his interactions with colleagues and clients became more open and charismatic. His new personal image reflected an innovative and approachable leader, someone who not only had experience but was also in tune with modern times.

This change had a ripple effect on his professional journey. John started receiving offers for more dynamic and creative projects, was invited to speak at industry conferences, and expanded his professional network significantly. His new personal image had opened doors to opportunities that once seemed out of reach.

In retrospect, John attributed a significant part of his renewed success to the work done with the image consultant. It wasn't just a matter of new clothes; it was a reawakening of his personal and professional identity, an alignment of his external image with his true inner self. John's story is a compelling example of how a change in personal image can be the catalyst for a broader transformation in a person's life.

Case Study 2: Stella's Metamorphosis in the Creative Field

Stella, a young and talented graphic designer, worked in a leading design studio. Despite her incredible talent and innovative ideas, Stella often felt overlooked and underestimated in her work environment. Her personal style, which leaned towards casual and at times disheveled clothing, prevented her from conveying her true competence and creative spirit.

The breakthrough came when Stella decided to collaborate with an image consultant, initially to prepare for an important design presentation. The consultant, after carefully listening to Stella's personal and professional story, understood that an approach was needed to enhance her creative personality without sacrificing professionalism.

Together, they decided to revamp Stella's wardrobe with a focus on garments that blended art and fashion. They introduced bold and artistic elements, such as custom graphic prints and modern accessories, that reflected her creative spirit. At the same time, they chose clothing with clean and sophisticated cuts to convey a sense of professionalism and maturity.

As her wardrobe evolved, Stella's self-esteem began to flourish. Each new outfit was a step forward in accepting her transformed body and an affirmation of her identity. Stella began to feel more confident in her daily interactions and work meetings. Her new image was a celebration of her resilience and strength, allowing her to present herself to the world with renewed confidence.

This transformation had a significant impact on her personal and professional life. During the presentation, Stella achieved great success, attracting the attention not only of her superiors but also of external clients. She began receiving offers for high-profile projects and became a prominent figure in the studio.

But the most significant change was internal. Stella felt more in tune with her professional and personal identity. Her new style was not just a means to be noticed but a way to express her true essence. Through collaboration with the image consultant, Stella had found a way to showcase her talent, opening up new opportunities and gaining the respect she deserved.

Stella's story is a vivid example of how a carefully curated image can serve as a springboard for professional success, especially in a field where creative expression is essential. Her transformation was not just a change of clothes but a revolution in her presence in the world of design.

Case Study 3: Dany's Rebirth

Dany, a successful manager in the technology sector, had gone through an extremely challenging period. After a long battle with health issues that led to significant weight loss, she found herself navigating a sea of uncertainties. Looking in the mirror, she could no longer recognize the woman reflected before her. Her old clothes, once a symbol of a confident and established professional image, now hung loose and inadequate, constant reminders of a difficult chapter in her life.

The decision to consult an image consultant was the first step in her transformation. Initially, Dany was hesitant, but the consultant, with a combination of sensitivity and professional expertise, quickly gained her trust. Together, they embarked on a journey of self-discovery that went beyond simply selecting a new wardrobe.

The consultant worked carefully with Dany to understand not only her new physical needs but also her desire to renew her personal and professional image. It was a process that required time and patience but gradually brought forth a revitalized Dany. They introduced garments that not only fit her new physique but also reflected her vibrant and dynamic personality: tailored outfits that emphasized her body's lines, bright colors that mirrored her energy, and accessories that added a touch of elegance and modernity.

As her wardrobe transformed, so did her self-esteem. Each new outfit was a step toward accepting her transformed body and affirming her identity. Dany began to feel more confident in her daily interactions and work meetings. Her new image was a celebration of her resilience and strength, allowing her to present herself to the world with renewed confidence.

This transformation had a cathartic impact on her personal and professional life. Dany not only regained her place in the professional world with greater strength and determination but also rediscovered the joy of socializing and participating in events, which she had neglected during her illness.

Dany's story is a powerful example of how rediscovering one's appearance can be a crucial part of the healing and personal growth process. Through collaboration with the image consultant, Dany not only changed her wardrobe but also reclaimed a sense of self that had eluded her. Her rebirth through image became a symbol of her new life, rich in hope, joy, and renewed self-confidence.

These case studies reflect real-life scenarios in which the intervention of an image consultant had a significant impact. They underscore how personal image is deeply intertwined with our self-perception, career, and emotional well-being, and how an experienced consultant can guide us on a journey of self-transformation and self-discovery.

FREQUENTLY ASKED QUESTIONS: WHAT ARE THE MAIN RESPONSIBILITIES OF AN IMAGE CONSULTANT?

The primary responsibilities of an image consultant span various areas, all centered around optimizing the client's personal image. Here are some of the frequently asked questions that help outline these responsibilities:

What is the main task of an image consultant?

The main task of an image consultant is to assist clients in developing and maintaining a personal image that aligns with their goals, whether they are professional, social, or personal. This includes clothing choices, accessories, grooming, and even body language and posture.

How does an image consultant personalize services for each client?

Image consultants conduct a thorough analysis of each client's needs, lifestyle, personal preferences, and goals. They use this information to create tailored advice that reflects the client's unique identity.

Do image consultants only focus on clothing?

No, their work goes beyond clothing. They also address aspects such as grooming, makeup, accessory selection, and may provide advice on body language and non-verbal communication to ensure an overall cohesive and authentic presentation.

Can an image consultant help improve self-confidence?

Yes, by working on building an image that positively and authentically reflects the client's personality, image consultants can help improve self-confidence and self-esteem.

What is the role of an image consultant in a career change or professional advancement?

In these scenarios, an image consultant helps the client develop an image that aligns with new professional goals, ensuring that the external image effectively communicates the client's professional skills and qualities.

Do image consultants follow fashion trends?

While it is important for an image consultant to stay updated on fashion trends, their primary goal is to adapt these trends to the unique needs and personality of the client, rather than blindly adhering to current fashion.

These frequently asked questions reflect the wide range of responsibilities that an image consultant must handle, highlighting the complexity and depth of their role in enhancing and transforming their clients' personal image.

DEBUNKING MYTHS: AN IMAGE CONSULTANT IS ONLY NEEDED FOR SPECIAL OCCASIONS

In the world of personal image and style, there is a common myth that portrays an image consultant as someone to be called upon only for special occasions, such as weddings, gala events, or significant professional presentations. However, this belief significantly diminishes the role and value that these professionals can bring to anyone's daily life.

The work of an image consultant is deeply rooted in the art of understanding and enhancing the uniqueness of each individual, regardless of the occasion. This professional is not limited to preparing clients for the spotlight of grand events; their true talent shines in the ability to weave personal image into the daily fabric of a person's life, making it a constant and dynamic element of expression and self-realization.

An image consultant immerses themselves in the client's life, exploring not only their stylistic preferences but also their lifestyle, personality, aspirations, and goals. This process allows the consultant to build a wardrobe that is not merely a collection of fashionable clothes but a true arsenal of self-expression.

Whether it's dressing for a typical day at the office, a coffee date with friends, a romantic evening, or a relaxing weekend, the consultant guides the client toward choices that are not only aesthetically pleasing but also tell a story – the story of who that person truly is. In this way, each selected garment becomes a statement of identity, a choice that goes beyond dressing to impress others but becomes a way of honoring oneself.

The personalized and intimate approach of an image consultant goes beyond clothing selection. Often, this work includes advice on how to pair clothing with the right accessories, how to experiment with different styles for various occasions, and how to adapt personal image to the changing circumstances of life, such as a career change, a new phase in personal life, or even a renewal after a health challenge.

This ongoing collaborative process between the client and the consultant creates a bond that goes beyond the professional. It becomes a relationship based on trust and understanding, where the consultant acts almost as a visual storyteller, helping the client tell their personal story through style and image.

Ultimately, the work of an image consultant is a celebration of individuality in every aspect of life. With a keen eye for detail and a deep understanding of human essence, these professionals transform the act of dressing into an expression of life, ensuring that every day is an opportunity to express who we truly are.

In the diverse fabric of the art of image consulting, their masterful touch extends beyond clothing selection, infiltrating every fiber of the client's daily existence. These professionals, with keen insight and profound intuition, are dedicated to shaping an overall image that goes beyond surface aesthetics.

Their work intertwines with aspects such as grooming and makeup, transforming these daily routines into acts of personal expression that reveal and celebrate the individual's uniqueness. However, the role of an image consultant does not stop here. Their skill extends to the subtle art of body language and posture, where every gesture, every movement becomes an additional word in the vocabulary of their personal expression.

With skillful guidance, they help clients embody a confidence rooted not only in their appearance but in their very presence – a confidence that permeates every room they enter, every encounter they have.

This aesthetic transformation, however, is balanced by an approach that values sustainability and timelessness. Far from being swept up by the fleeting currents of passing fashion, image consultants guide their clients toward a wardrobe that is not only stylish and refined but also stands the test of time. They select garments that not only fit various occasions but can be worn and cherished for years, creating a style that is both practical and personal.

And in times of transition – whether it's career advancements, physical changes, or evolutions in lifestyle – the image consultant becomes a beacon of stability and understanding. They guide their clients through these turbulent waters, ensuring that the image they present to the world remains true to their evolving essence. In this process, the image consultant is more than just a stylist or a fashion expert; they become a companion on the client's journey, a guardian of their image that helps them navigate life's changes with grace and confidence.

In summary, an image consultant is not a luxury reserved only for extraordinary occasions but a strategic partner in building a personal image that accompanies and enhances the individual in all aspects of their life. Their expertise and touch can transform not only how a person appears but, more profoundly, how they feel and move in the world.

THE PERSONAL SHOPPER

In the vibrant and dynamic world of fashion and personal style, the figure of the personal shopper emerges as an expert and intuitive guide, a professional whose role goes far beyond simply choosing clothes and accessories. This style expert does not limit themselves to a superficial approach to fashion; instead, they delve into the depths of the client's personality and individual needs, providing a service that combines fashion expertise with a keen understanding of the individual.

A personal shopper, with their extensive knowledge of current trends, seasonal collections, and the best places for shopping, dedicates themselves to finding items that are not only fashionable but also perfectly aligned with the client's style, preferences, and budget. Their work does not stop at selecting a piece of clothing that fits well; it is a more complex and mature process aimed at creating a tailored, efficient, and rewarding shopping experience.

The approach of the personal shopper is deeply personalized. They strive to understand the client on a personal level, exploring their lifestyle, personal tastes, and aspirations. This work translates into a shopping journey that is more than just a transaction; it becomes a true exploration of personal style, where every choice is a step toward self-affirmation.

In addition to selecting clothing for the everyday wardrobe or special events, the personal shopper can also undertake the client's style transformation, guiding them through an image change that reflects a new phase in their life or a change in their personal journey. This process of transformation is not only practical but also an emotional and self-discovery journey for the client.

In some cases, the role of the personal shopper extends beyond the world of fashion. They can become a lifestyle consultant, selecting home items, gifts, and organizing experiences that align with the client's interests and preferences. In this capacity, the personal shopper becomes a curator of experiences, an expert who helps the client navigate a world of choices to find those that best reflect their personality and lifestyle.

In conclusion, the personal shopper is much more than just a shopping assistant; they are an artist of personal taste, a master in creating an image that is authentic and representative of the client. Through their work, they not only help clients enhance their wardrobe but also develop greater self-confidence in themselves and their style choices, transforming how they present themselves and perceive themselves in the world.

DIFFERENCES BETWEEN PERSONAL SHOPPERS AND IMAGE CONSULTANTS

Often, the roles of a personal shopper and an image consultant are misconstrued, with some considering them almost interchangeable. However, although both are focused on personal image and style, their functions, skills, and approaches are distinct and complementary.

Personal Shopper: The Master of Personalized Shopping

The personal shopper, an undisputed master of personalized shopping, embodies the quintessential style consultant. Their expertise extends beyond mere knowledge of fashion trends to a profound understanding of individual needs, personal preferences, and idiosyncrasies. This professional transforms the shopping experience from a routine or sometimes stressful activity into an exclusive and personalized adventure, geared towards uncovering hidden treasures in the vast world of fashion.

Expert Navigator of the Fashion World

The personal shopper navigates effortlessly between exclusive boutiques, department stores, and online shops, maneuvering through a myriad of brands, collections, and designers. Their knowledge runs deep; they know the history behind each brand, the quality of materials, the craftsmanship of each garment, and most importantly, they can recognize those unique pieces that can enrich the client's wardrobe significantly.

An Eye for Personal Style and Practical Needs

The true magic of a personal shopper lies in their ability to align fashion trends with each client's unique personal style. Far from pushing for ephemeral or impractical purchases, this professional seeks to understand the client's lifestyle, preferences, and practical needs, guiding them towards choices that are not only visually pleasing but also functional and versatile.

Beyond the Wardrobe: A Lifestyle Consultant

While the core of the personal shopper's work is clothing, their role often extends beyond that. They can advise on accessories, jewelry, and even elements contributing to an overall image, such as fragrances or design items that reflect the client's style and taste. Their skill in grasping and interpreting the client's desires makes them well-rounded style consultants.

A Tailored Service for Every Client

The personal shopper is particularly valuable for those with hectic lifestyles, constant professional commitments, or those who simply want to avoid the hassle and confusion of traditional shopping. Working one-on-one with the client, this professional customizes each shopping experience, saving precious time and reducing stress, all while ensuring that every purchase is well-considered and perfectly aligned with the client's needs.

In conclusion, the personal shopper represents an indispensable guide in the world of fashion and personal style, an ally who transforms shopping into an exclusive, enjoyable, and, above all, personalized experience. Through their intervention, clients not only enhance their wardrobe but also elevate their style experience, learning to make more conscious fashion choices that align with their true essence.

Image Consultant: The Architect of Personal Image

The image consultant, a key figure in the realm of personal style, operates with a decidedly holistic approach compared to the personal shopper. This professional goes beyond selecting clothing pieces that fit the client physically and stylistically; their mission is to build, refine, and enhance the entire image of the client, turning it into a tangible reflection of their personality, values, and aspirations.

A Holistic Approach to Personal Image

The image consultant delves deeper, immersing themselves in the client's personality. This means understanding not only aesthetic tastes but also life goals, professional ambitions, and how the client intends to present themselves to the world. This in-depth analysis allows the consultant to develop an image strategy that perfectly aligns with the client's life and objectives.

Work on Multidimensional Aspects of Image

Beyond clothing, the image consultant refines aspects like grooming, makeup, and hairstyle. These details, though they may seem minor, are crucial in creating a coherent and polished image. A well-chosen haircut, for instance, can transform a person's appearance, just as suitable makeup can enhance distinctive features and reflect mood or occasion.

Posture and Body Language: Key Components of Image

An often overlooked but vital aspect of personal image is posture and body language. The image consultant works with the client to develop a bearing that exudes confidence and authority. Correct body language not only improves physical appearance but also influences how others perceive us.

Boosting Self-Esteem Through Image

One of the primary goals of the image consultant is to boost the client's self-esteem. Having an image that truly reflects who you are can significantly impact self-perception and self-confidence. The consultant helps clients feel comfortable and confident in their appearance, promoting an overall sense of well-being.

Effective Communication of Identity and Values

Ultimately, the image consultant aims to create an image that effectively communicates the client's identity and values. In an increasingly visual world, the image we project can speak volumes before a single word is uttered. A well-groomed and authentic image can open doors and create opportunities in both personal and professional life.

In summary, the image consultant is an artist and communicator of personal image, an expert who uses their knowledge not only to enhance aesthetics but to transform image into a powerful tool of personal and professional expression. Through their work, image consultants help clients navigate the world with greater confidence, elegance, and authenticity.

Key Differences and Synergies

The differences between the personal shopper and the image consultant lie not only in their specific skills but also in how they approach the transformation of the client's personal image. While both make significant contributions to image and style, their methods and goals tend to differ, although there is some intersection and potential for collaboration.

The Personal Shopper: Expert in Targeted Shopping

The personal shopper, with their specialization in shopping, primarily focuses on the most tangible aspect of the image - the wardrobe. This professional strives to find clothing and accessories that not only fit the client's style and body perfectly but also meet their daily practical needs. It's a more immediate and concrete approach, often sought by clients who need to quickly update their wardrobe or seek assistance with specific purchases. The personal shopper is a valuable ally for those seeking efficiency, time savings, and targeted fashion shopping advice.

The Image Consultant: The Architect of Holistic Image

On the other hand, the image consultant takes a holistic and long-term approach. Their work extends beyond clothing selection, encompassing aspects such as grooming, makeup, posture, body language, and even social etiquette. Through a process that can last for weeks or months, the image consultant works closely with the client to develop and refine an image that authentically communicates their personality and values. This journey often involves inner work, aiming to boost self-esteem and self-confidence through a more coherent and polished external presentation.

Synergies and Collaboration

Despite their differences, personal shoppers and image consultants can work in synergy. For example, a client who has worked with an image consultant to define their personal image and style may subsequently turn to a personal shopper to concretely implement the advice received, purchasing clothing that perfectly fits the new image. Similarly, a client starting their journey with a personal shopper may discover the need for more in-depth work on their image and style, then turning to an image consultant for a more holistic analysis.

In conclusion, while personal shoppers and image consultants have distinct roles and approaches in the world of fashion and personal image, both play a crucial role in guiding clients toward an image that reflects their true essence. Their collaboration can lead to a complete transformation of the client's style and image, combining the practical and tangible aspects of shopping with a deeper and more reflective approach to personal presentation.

EVALUATION OF CUSTOMER NEEDS AND PREFERENCES

In the process of enhancing personal image, both the personal shopper and the image consultant pay special attention to evaluating the needs and preferences of their clients. This aspect is fundamental to ensure that the services provided not only align with the client's expectations but also help them express their unique personality through style.

In-Depth Understanding of the Client

The starting point for both professionals is a deep understanding of the client. This includes a detailed discussion of style preferences, personal interests, lifestyle, professional and social needs, as well as the client's specific expectations and goals in terms of their image. During this process, various factors such as age, body type, skin color, and hair color are taken into account to ensure that every suggestion is tailored to the client.

Analysis of Style and Tastes

A crucial aspect of this process is the analysis of the client's current style and tastes. This helps determine which elements of their current style work well and which could be improved. The personal shopper or image consultant may also ask clients to share images of styles they admire or aspire to emulate, providing a solid foundation for future recommendations.

Adaptation to Practical Needs

Another important aspect is adapting to the practical needs of the client. For example, a professional working in a corporate environment will have different needs than a freelance artist. The image consultant or personal shopper assesses these aspects to ensure that the wardrobe and overall image are not only aesthetically pleasing but also practical and functional for the client's daily life.

Continuous Feedback and Adaptation

Assessing the needs and preferences of clients is an ongoing process. Both professional figures remain open to client feedback and are ready to adapt their services to changing needs or preferences. This dynamic approach ensures that clients feel heard and understood, and that the services provided remain relevant and satisfying over time.

In summary, evaluating the needs and preferences of clients is a cornerstone of the work of both the personal shopper and the image consultant. Through careful analysis and attentive listening, these professionals are able to create personalized style solutions that not only enhance the client's external image but also reflect and enhance their internal identity.

FREQUENTLY ASKED QUESTIONS: WHAT SERVICES DOES A PERSONAL SHOPPER OFFER?

The personal shopper, as a specialized professional in the field of fashion and shopping, offers a variety of services that go well beyond simply selecting clothing. Their expertise extends to different areas, all aimed at optimizing the shopping experience and the client's style. Here are some frequently asked questions that outline the services typically offered by a personal shopper:

What exactly does a personal shopper do?

A personal shopper helps clients choose and purchase clothing and accessories. Their service includes selecting garments that fit the client's style, needs, and budget, providing advice on colors, cuts, and fashion trends.

Can I use a personal shopper for special occasions?

Absolutely. Many clients turn to personal shoppers to find the right clothing for special events such as weddings, formal parties, or job interviews. The personal shopper ensures that the client is dressed appropriately and stylishly for the occasion.

Can a personal shopper help me refresh my wardrobe?

Yes, one of the main services offered by a personal shopper is assistance in refreshing the wardrobe. This can include evaluating the client's existing clothing and recommending new items to update and revitalize their style.

Do personal shoppers offer style consultations?

Many personal shoppers offer style consultations where they discuss the client's preferences, analyze their body type, and provide advice on how to dress to best accentuate their figure.

Can I use a personal shopper for online shopping?

Yes, with the increase in online shopping, many personal shoppers offer virtual consulting services. They can recommend items online, organize orders, and even assist with returns.

Can a personal shopper accompany me during shopping?

Certainly. Some personal shoppers offer personalized shopping companionship services, selecting stores that match the client's taste and budget and providing real-time advice.

Do personal shoppers only work with wealthy and famous clients?

No, this is a common myth. Personal shoppers are accessible to a wide range of clients, regardless of their budget. Many offer flexible packages and services tailored to each client's financial needs.

Can they help me find deals and discounts?

Yes, one of the advantages of using a personal shopper is their ability to find the best deals and discounts. Thanks to their industry and store knowledge, they can help clients get the most value for their purchases.

In summary, the services offered by a personal shopper are diverse and customized to meet the client's style, budget, and daily life needs. From a simple style consultation to a complete wardrobe makeover, the personal shopper is an invaluable resource for anyone looking to enhance their shopping experience and personal style.

MYTHS TO DEBUNK: A PERSONAL SHOPPER IS ONLY FOR THE WEALTHY AND FAMOUS

Contrary to popular belief, the idea that a personal shopper is a luxury reserved exclusively for the wealthy and famous is significantly misleading. This perception often stems from the image of an elitist and inaccessible fashion world, but in reality, the personal shopper service is much more democratic and widespread than one might think. In everyday life, these fashion professionals offer their services to a diverse clientele, not limited by social status or astronomical bank accounts.

In fact, a personal shopper caters to anyone looking for a style update, support in shopping, or guidance through ever-changing fashion trends. This service is particularly valuable for those with daily commitments that leave little time for shopping, such as busy professionals, parents, or individuals who simply do not find pleasure in wandering through stores. The assistance of a personal shopper can transform what could be a potentially stressful and time-consuming experience into an efficient, enjoyable, and focused process.

Furthermore, the idea that personal shoppers only promote luxury purchases is another misunderstanding. Many of these professionals are experts in finding deals, quality items at affordable prices, and building versatile wardrobes that maximize the client's investment. Their goal is often to create a sustainable and timeless wardrobe that transcends passing fashions and provides lasting value, regardless of the budget.

The advancement of technology and the popularity of online shopping have further opened the doors to broader access to personal shopping services. With virtual consultations and online shopping, personal shoppers can now reach a wider clientele, offering personalized advice without the need for face-to-face meetings or exorbitant budgets.

A personal shopper, therefore, is not just a luxury for the chosen few but an accessible partner in creating and maintaining a personal style that reflects an individual's personality and needs. These professionals offer value beyond mere clothing purchases: they provide guidance for self-expression through fashion, making this service valuable and relevant to a wide range of people. In this way, the personal shopper democratizes style, making it a joy and possibility for everyone, not just for an exclusive circle of elites.

NON-VERBAL COMMUNICATION

Non-verbal Communication: An Essential Aspect of Human Expression

Non-verbal communication is a fundamental aspect of human expression that plays a crucial role in how we interact with others and how we are perceived. It encompasses a wide range of signals and behaviors that go beyond words, including body language, facial expression, eye contact, posture, gestures, and even clothing and physical appearance.

Body Language and Posture

Posture and body language are perhaps the most immediately recognizable elements of non-verbal communication. An upright and open posture can convey confidence and openness, while a closed or slouched posture may suggest insecurity or defensiveness. Gestures, such as how we move our hands while speaking or how we maintain distance from others, also communicate subtle messages about our intentions, feelings, and reactions.

Facial Expressions and Eye Contact

Facial expressions are another key component of non-verbal communication, often revealing emotions and reactions more honestly than words. Smiles, furrowed brows, blushing—all convey significant information. Eye contact, in particular, is essential in human communication; it can indicate interest, attention, trust, or, conversely, discomfort and uncertainty.

Clothing and Physical Appearance

Clothing and physical appearance, though often overlooked, are powerful tools of non-verbal communication. How we choose to present ourselves through our style, clothing, and grooming can significantly influence how others perceive us. These elements can reflect our personality, status, social group, and even our aspirations.

Importance in Social and Professional Life

In both social and professional life, understanding and effectively controlling non-verbal communication are essential. For example, in a job interview or a business meeting, proper non-verbal communication can reinforce the verbal message and create an impression of competence and reliability. Similarly, in personal life, being aware of non-verbal cues can improve relationships and social interactions.

Learning and Adaptation

Non-verbal communication is not always intuitive; it can vary greatly across different cultures and social environments. Therefore, it is important to learn to interpret and adapt one's non-verbal behavior based on the context. This includes being aware of one's own non-verbal signals and understanding how they can be interpreted by others.

In conclusion, non-verbal communication is a complex and powerful aspect of human communication. It plays a fundamental role in how we express ourselves, interpret others, and build relationships. Mastery of non-verbal communication can significantly enhance both our personal and professional interactions, making us more effective and aware communicators.

THE INFLUENCE OF CLOTHING IN COMMUNICATION

Clothing, often perceived simply as a necessity or a form of personal expression, actually plays a fundamental role in non-verbal communication. The choice of what to wear every day is much more than an aesthetic decision; it is a silent yet extremely eloquent form of communication that can profoundly influence how we perceive ourselves and how others perceive us.

When we select an outfit, we are unconsciously selecting a language through which we convey messages to the external world. Every piece of clothing, from its color to its style, from its formality to its uniqueness, communicates a set of information about who we are, our social status, our preferences, and even our mood. In professional settings, for example, formal and well-groomed attire can communicate professionalism, reliability, and respect for the situation and the people involved. In more casual contexts, clothing can express our personality, passions, and approach to life.

Similarly, clothing can function as an extension of our personal identity. In many cases, what we choose to wear becomes an integral part of how we express our individuality and uniqueness. Fashion, in this sense, becomes a tool through which we can express our creativity, mood, values, and aspirations. For example, wearing clothes that reflect the latest trends can communicate an interest in modernity and current trends, while choosing vintage or eclectic attire can express an appreciation for individuality and diversity.

However, clothing can also be a source of misunderstandings or prejudices. First impressions, often based on outward appearance, can lead to assumptions about a person's personality, abilities, or background. This underscores the importance of choosing clothing consciously, taking into account the message we want to convey and the context in which we find ourselves.

Furthermore, clothing can influence not only how we are perceived by others but also how we perceive ourselves. The phenomenon known as "enclothed cognition" suggests that the clothes we wear can impact our psychological state and performance. For example, wearing clothes we consider professional and appropriate can boost our confidence in work-related situations, while wearing comfortable and relaxed attire can help us feel more at ease in casual settings.

In conclusion, clothing is a powerful tool of non-verbal communication that goes far beyond mere functionality or aesthetics. It is a means through which we tell our story, express our personality, and navigate the various social spheres of our lives. Understanding and consciously using the power of clothing in communication can enrich our social interactions, improve our self-perception, and allow us to express who we are more fully.

PRACTICAL EXAMPLES AND TIPS

Clothing as a tool of non-verbal communication offers endless possibilities to express one's identity and influence others' perception. Here are some practical examples and tips on how to harness the power of clothing in everyday life:

In a Professional Setting: In a work context, wearing clothes that align with the company culture and reflect professionalism can help create a good first impression. For example, for a job interview, opting for a tailored suit or a pantsuit can convey seriousness and attention to detail. Even in less formal work environments, choosing clean, tidy attire that reflects a certain degree of professionalism can help establish authority and competence.

In Social Life: For social events like dinners or informal gatherings, clothing can be used to express one's personality. For instance, a colorful outfit or a unique accessory can be great ways to showcase your personal style and spark conversations. However, it's important to consider the context and the event's atmosphere to avoid appearing overly casual or formal.

On Special Occasions: For events such as weddings, parties, or ceremonies, clothing plays a crucial role in adhering to the event's protocol and etiquette. Inquiring about the dress code in advance and choosing an appropriate outfit demonstrates respect for the occasion and fellow attendees.

Boosting Self-Esteem: Clothing can significantly influence our self-esteem and self-confidence. Wearing garments that make us feel comfortable, flatter our figure, and reflect our personal style can enhance confidence and overall well-being. A useful exercise can be to wear an item of clothing that is normally considered "too bold" or "outside one's comfort zone" to experiment with how it affects one's mood.

Adapting to Body Changes: Clothing can also be adapted to highlight changes in the body, such as weight loss or gain. Choosing clothes that fit well with one's current body shape, rather than trying to fit into old garments, can contribute to a positive body image and personal satisfaction.

Maintaining a Versatile Wardrobe: Having a versatile wardrobe composed of easily combinable basic pieces can simplify daily clothing choices and ensure that you always have something suitable to wear for any occasion. Investing in quality and timeless clothing items, rather than blindly following fashion trends, can lead to a more personal and enduring style.

In summary, clothing is much more than simply covering the body; it is a form of personal expression and a powerful tool of non-verbal communication. Using it consciously and intentionally can bring benefits both in professional and social life, enhancing others' perception and boosting self-confidence.

FREQUENTLY ASKED QUESTIONS: HOW CAN CLOTHING ENHANCE NON-VERBAL COMMUNICATION?

Clothing, as a significant aspect of non-verbal communication, can enhance it in several ways. Here are some frequently asked questions that explore how clothing influences this form of communication:

How can clothing influence the first impression?

Clothing is often one of the first details that others notice. Dressing appropriately and neatly can create a positive first impression, conveying professionalism, confidence, and attention to detail. This is particularly important in contexts such as job interviews or business meetings.

Can clothing reflect personality?

Absolutely. The garments we choose to wear can express aspects of our personality, such as creativity, practicality, fashion awareness, or a preference for comfort. Through clothing, we can communicate who we are without the need for words.

Can clothing influence self-confidence?

Yes, what we wear can have a significant impact on our self-esteem and confidence. Wearing clothes in which we feel comfortable and that we consider flattering can boost our confidence, which in turn enhances our body language and overall presence.

How can clothing communicate respect?

Choosing appropriate clothing for a specific occasion shows

respect for the events and people involved. For example, wearing formal attire for an important event or adhering to a company's dress code demonstrates a commitment to honoring social or professional conventions.

Can clothing influence perceived authority?

Wearing clothing associated with professionalism and power, such as a well-tailored suit or an elegant pantsuit, can enhance perceived authority. This can be particularly useful in workplace settings or situations where establishing credibility is important.

Is it possible to use clothing to adapt to different cultural contexts?

Absolutely. Being aware of cultural norms related to clothing and adapting one's style accordingly can facilitate communication and interaction in different cultural contexts. It demonstrates respect and sensitivity to the traditions and customs of others.

In summary, clothing is a powerful tool of non-verbal communication that can significantly improve how we are perceived and how we perceive ourselves. The conscious choice of clothing and accessories can enhance our communication in many contexts, positively influencing first impressions, confidence, respect, perceived authority, and cultural adaptability.

DEBUNKING MYTHS: NON-VERBAL COMMUNICATION IS LESS IMPORTANT THAN WORDS

Contrary to a fairly widespread myth, non-verbal communication is often just as, if not more, important than the words we use. Our society tends to place great importance on verbal language, the chosen words, and how they are pronounced. However, non-verbal communication - which includes body language, facial expressions, eye contact, posture, and even clothing - conveys a wealth of information that can prove crucial in understanding the overall message.

Research in the field of communication suggests that a significant percentage of communication between individuals occurs at a non-verbal level. This means that even when we are not speaking, we are constantly communicating through our behaviors, posture, expressions, and physical presence.

For example, let's consider the impact of posture: a person who stands upright and maintains eye contact during a conversation can convey confidence and openness, while an inability to maintain eye contact or a closed posture may suggest insecurity, disinterest, or even hostility. These non-verbal signals can modulate or even contradict the verbal message, significantly influencing the listener's perception.

Similarly, facial expressions can communicate a wide range of emotions and reactions, sometimes more honestly than the words themselves. A genuine smile can convey warmth and welcome, while a puzzled or worried expression may raise doubts about the sincerity of what is being said verbally.

Furthermore, clothing and physical appearance play a fundamental role in non-verbal communication. The choice of clothing, how it is worn, the cleanliness, and orderliness of attire can convey messages related to a person's personality, social status, professionalism, and even mood.

Non-verbal communication is, therefore, an essential aspect of human interaction. Understanding and correctly using it can significantly enhance the quality of our communication, allowing us to convey our messages more effectively and interpret those of others more accurately. Debunking the myth that non-verbal communication is less important than words is fundamental for a full understanding and mastery of communicative dynamics.

THE FASHION MARKET AND CONSUMER PSYCHOLOGY

The fashion market and consumer psychology are closely intertwined, creating a fascinating landscape where psychology, economics, and culture merge. When exploring this field, one encounters a complex interplay of desires, perceptions, and strategies that influence both consumers and fashion creators.

At the core of the fashion market lies consumer psychology, a field that studies how and why consumers choose specific fashion products. This choice is not merely a matter of necessity or aesthetic preference but is deeply rooted in complex psychological processes. Consumers are influenced by a variety of factors, from personal identity to the quest for belonging to a group, from the expression of status and wealth to the desire to stand out from others.

Fashion trends, for example, are a powerful illustration of how consumer psychology operates in the market. Trends can emerge as an expression of a collective need for novelty or as a response to cultural or social changes. Once a trend gains popularity, it triggers a social conformity phenomenon where consumers purchase certain products to feel part of a group or to be perceived as keeping up with the times.

Simultaneously, fashion serves as a tool for self-expression. Individuals choose specific styles to communicate aspects of their personality or to convey specific messages. This aspect of consumer psychology highlights the desire for uniqueness and individuality that can often coexist with the tendency toward conformity.

Furthermore, the psychology behind fashion purchasing decisions is influenced by factors such as marketing and advertising. Advertising campaigns that evoke emotions, aspirations, and ideals can significantly impact purchasing decisions. Marketing strategies that leverage celebrities, influencers, or compelling narratives can create a strong desire for certain products or brands, guiding consumers towards specific choices.

The role of social media in the fashion market is another relevant aspect of consumer psychology. Platforms like Instagram and TikTok have transformed how consumers interact with fashion, providing immediate access to the latest trends and influencing purchasing decisions through the sharing of images and videos.

Finally, sustainability is becoming an increasingly important factor in fashion purchasing decisions. Consumers, increasingly aware of the environmental and social impact of fashion, are beginning to prefer brands that adopt sustainable practices. This shift reflects a growing social and environmental consciousness and is reshaping the fashion market landscape.

In summary, the fashion market is a complex ecosystem where consumer psychology plays a crucial role. Understanding these psychological mechanisms is essential not only for brands and designers seeking to understand and influence consumer behaviors but also offers consumers themselves greater awareness of the forces influencing their fashion choices.

In analyzing the current trends in the fashion market, we find a rich and multifaceted landscape characterized by a continuous flow of new ideas, cultural influences, and responses to social changes. This dynamism makes the fashion industry not only a fertile ground for stylistic innovation but also a mirror reflecting the transformations and aspirations of society.

At the heart of this vibrant scenario, there is an increasingly pronounced trend toward sustainability and ethical awareness in fashion consumption. This inclination is no longer a subtle background in the fashion discourse but has become a dominant force reshaping the industry's landscape. The rise of environmental awareness and growing concern for the ethical implications of fashion production are pushing both consumers and brands to reconsider their choices and practices.

Consumers, becoming more informed due to easier access to information, are becoming key players in this change. Their demand for transparency, environmental responsibility, and fairness in the production process is profoundly influencing how brands approach fashion production. This shift in focus manifests in various ways, from an increase in the production of garments using recycled or sustainable materials to the adoption of production processes that reduce environmental impact, to rethinking the lifecycle of fashion products.

Sustainability, in this context, is no longer seen as an option or niche choice but as a strategic imperative driving innovation in the industry. Major brands and fashion houses are integrating sustainability principles into their collections, not only to respond to market demands but also to position themselves as responsible leaders in a transforming industry. This is reflected in the adoption of eco-friendly materials, the promotion of conscious consumption practices, and the quest for solutions to reduce waste at all stages of the fashion value chain.

Furthermore, this push toward sustainability is also influencing the perception and value of fashion products. Consumers are beginning to assess items not only based on their aesthetic appeal or brand but also based on their environmental and social impact. This change is leading to a new evaluation of luxury, where quality, ethics, and sustainability have become as important as style and design.

In conclusion, the current trend toward sustainability and ethical awareness in the fashion market represents a vital response to the socio-cultural changes of our time. This evolution is shaping not only the appearance of the fashion industry but also its ethical core and its relationship with society and the environment. In this dynamic context, fashion becomes a means to express not only personal style but also values and principles, marking a significant step toward a more responsible and aware future.

The digitization of the fashion industry represents one of the most significant and impactful transformations in recent years. With the rise of online shopping, particularly accelerated by the circumstances imposed by the global pandemic, there has been a radical shift in purchasing habits. This move towards digital has prompted fashion brands to rethink and innovate their strategies, quickly adapting to an increasingly connected and technologically advanced landscape.

At the core of this digital evolution, we find an increasingly sophisticated and technology-oriented approach to fashion marketing. Brands are exploring and implementing solutions like augmented reality to provide immersive virtual shopping experiences, allowing customers to virtually try on clothing and accessories in a digital environment. These technologies not only enrich the online shopping experience but also open new possibilities for customer interaction and engagement.

Social media has played a fundamental role in this digital transition. Platforms like Instagram, TikTok, and Pinterest have become true digital showcases, where brands not only present their products but also create and spread trends. The power of influencers and celebrities in shaping consumer perceptions and purchasing decisions is unmatched. Through posts, stories, and influencer-brand collaborations, fashion trends emerge and spread at an unprecedented pace.

In parallel with this digitization, we witness an interesting intersection of nostalgia and innovation in the fashion world. A wave of nostalgia has brought back vintage styles from the 1990s and 2000s, reimagined with a contemporary twist. This revival is not only a tribute to the past but also a creative exploration of how retro elements can be fused with contemporary trends to create something unique and current.

At the same time, the industry is pushing the boundaries of innovation. Designers and brands are exploring new materials, experimenting with bold cuts and unconventional shapes, challenging and redefining traditional fashion conventions. This desire for innovation is fueled by both technology and creativity, leading to the birth of styles that are as futuristic as they are rooted in fashion tradition.

In summary, the current fashion landscape is a fascinating blend of digitization and stylistic innovation. On one hand, technology is transforming how consumers interact with fashion and make purchasing decisions. On the other hand, a renewed interest in past trends and a bold exploration of new stylistic frontiers are driving the creative direction of the industry. In this dynamic context, fashion is not only a commercial phenomenon but also an ever-evolving expressive field, a place where the past, present, and future meet and merge in continually new and surprising ways.

In a world where uniqueness and authenticity are increasingly valued, personalization emerges as a key trend in the fashion market. Modern consumers are seeking products that not only meet their functional needs but also reflect their individuality and personal style. This push toward personalization is leading to a gradual but definitive shift from mass production to artisanal or bespoke production, a change that reflects the growing demand for uniqueness and originality.

In this context, personalized clothing is gaining ground, with an increasing number of brands offering custom or semi-custom options. These services allow customers to choose fabrics, cuts, colors, and details, creating garments that fit perfectly to their bodies and their style. But personalization goes beyond clothing; it is also touching accessories, footwear, and beauty products. This trend is reflected in the growing popularity of customizable jewelry, custom-made shoes, and cosmetics that can be tailored to an individual's specific skin needs.

In parallel, we are witnessing an interesting intersection between technology and design in the fashion industry. Technological innovation is pushing the boundaries of what is possible in fashion design, introducing high-tech fabrics and cutting-edge production techniques. These developments are not only revolutionizing how garments are created but also transforming their distribution and sale.

The use of digital technology, for example, allows brands to offer online customization experiences, where customers can virtually design their garments and see the final result before production. 3D printing and other emerging technologies are opening new possibilities in creating customized garments and accessories, reducing production times, and increasing precision.

Materials are also undergoing an evolution, with the development of innovative fabrics offering enhanced features such as sustainability, durability, and even integrated technological functionality. These advancements are leading to a new kind of fashion, where functionality, style, and personalization merge in unique and exciting ways.

Personalization in the fashion market reflects the growing demand for products that not only look beautiful and stylish but also tell the unique and personal story of the wearer. The intersection of technology and design is amplifying this trend, pushing the industry toward a future where fashion is not only personalized but also technologically advanced and deeply connected with the identity and lifestyle of consumers.

In summary, the current fashion market is characterized by an intriguing interplay of sustainability, technology, personalization, and stylistic reinterpretation. These elements, combined with changing consumer needs and expectations, are shaping a rapidly evolving industry where the ability to adapt and innovate is crucial for success in the global fashion market.

INFLUENCE OF PSYCHOLOGY ON PURCHASING DECISIONS

Psychology has a profound and multifaceted impact on purchasing decisions, influencing consumer behavior in ways that go far beyond simple assessments of product quality or price. This complex field intertwines elements of emotion, perception, motivation, and cognition to explain why people choose certain products or brands and how their experiences and environment influence those choices.

A fundamental element in the psychology of purchasing decisions is emotion. Consumer choices are often driven by feelings and emotional responses, sometimes more than by rational analysis. For example, the desire for belonging or the need to express one's identity can drive the purchase of specific brands or products. Brands that can create a strong emotional connection with consumers through engaging stories, evocative imagery, or shared values tend to have a greater impact on purchasing decisions.

Consumer perception is another critical aspect. This includes not only how the product itself is perceived but also the brand image, product presentation, and the environment in which it is sold. Visual presentation, scent, music, and store atmosphere, for instance, can strongly influence how consumers perceive products and, consequently, their purchasing decisions.

Motivation plays a crucial role in purchasing decisions. People buy products for a variety of reasons, ranging from satisfying basic needs like food and clothing to more complex needs such as social recognition or self-fulfillment. Understanding which motivations drive consumers toward certain products can help brands position themselves more effectively and develop targeted marketing strategies.

Another important aspect is the cognitive process behind

purchasing decisions. Consumers actively process information about products, compare alternatives, and assess risks and benefits. This process can be influenced by various factors, such as prior knowledge of the product, opinions of friends and family, or online reviews.

Finally, social and cultural influence cannot be underestimated. Purchasing decisions are often influenced by social trends, peer groups, cultural norms, and even mass phenomena. People can be influenced by what celebrities wear, what is popular in their social circles, or what is considered culturally desirable.

In conclusion, the psychology of purchasing decisions is a vast field that incorporates a range of emotional, perceptual, motivational, and cognitive processes. Understanding these aspects can offer valuable insights into why consumers behave as they do, enabling brands to develop more effective strategies and consumers to make more informed decisions.

FREQUENTLY ASKED QUESTIONS: HOW DO FASHION TRENDS CHANGE?

Fashion trends are constantly changing, evolving, and adapting in response to a variety of cultural, social, and economic influences. This fluidity of trends often raises questions about how and why they change. Here are some frequently asked questions that explore the ever-changing nature of fashion trends:

What determines the change in fashion trends?

Fashion trends change in response to a variety of factors. These can include cultural influences such as movies, music, art, and literature, social and economic changes, technological innovations, and even global events like a pandemic. Influential figures like celebrities, designers, and social media influencers also play a significant role in shaping and changing trends.

How often do fashion trends change?

Fashion trends can change at varying frequencies. Some trends can last for several seasons or even years, while others may be fleeting, lasting only a few months. The fashion industry, especially fast fashion, has accelerated the trend cycle, leading to more rapid and frequent changes.

How do social media influence fashion trends?

Social media has revolutionized how fashion trends spread and are adopted. Platforms like Instagram and TikTok allow trends to quickly reach a global audience, with influencers and content creators often serving as catalysts for new trends. These channels also enable greater consumer engagement and interaction with fashion.

Are fashion trends predictable?

Predicting fashion trends can be complex due to their ever-changing nature and the variety of factors influencing the industry. However, fashion experts and trend forecasters use a combination of data analysis, observation of cultural trends, and intuition to predict future fashion directions.

Do past trends come back?

Yes, fashion trends often follow cyclical patterns, with popular styles from the past returning in a refreshed form. This phenomenon, known as "retro fashion," sees styles from previous decades, such as the '70s, '80s, or '90s, being reinterpreted and updated for contemporary tastes.

Who determines new fashion trends?

New fashion trends are often set by a combination of influential designers, fashion houses, figures from the entertainment industry, and social media influencers. Fashion weeks, industry fairs, and new collection launch events are key moments where new trends are showcased.

In summary, fashion trends result from a complex interplay of cultural, social, and economic influences, as well as innovations in the fashion and design field. Their ever-evolving nature reflects the dynamism of human expression and changing consumer preferences.

MYTHS TO DEBUNK: FASHION TRENDS ARE THE SAME WORLDWIDE

The myth that fashion trends are uniform worldwide clashes with the rich variety and diversity that characterizes the global fashion landscape. While it is true that globalization and digital connectivity have contributed to spreading certain trends globally, it is equally true that the interpretation and adoption of these trends vary significantly based on multiple cultural, social, and geographical factors.

Fashion, by its nature, is an expression of culture. The traditions, values, and social norms of each country or region profoundly influence style choices and fashion preferences. For example, in some Asian countries, clothing can be strongly influenced by traditional aesthetic principles and contemporary pop culture, resulting in a style that blends traditional and modern elements uniquely. In contrast, in many Western cities, fashion may be more oriented towards individual expression and stylistic avant-garde.

Additionally, fashion in different parts of the world also responds to practical needs such as climate. In countries with cold and prolonged winter seasons, winter clothing like heavy coats and wool sweaters dominates fashion trends. In contrast, in tropical or equatorial regions, fashion tends to focus on lightweight, breathable, and colorful clothing suitable for hot and humid climates.

Another important aspect is the accessibility and availability of certain products. Popular trends in urban and metropolitan areas with easy access to a wide range of brands and stores may not be as present in more remote areas or in countries with limited access to these brands. This can lead to the development of unique local fashion scenes, where indigenous styles and local preferences take precedence.

Social media and digital fashion have had a significant impact on the spread of trends, but even in this area, there is great variety. While some global platforms like Instagram and Pinterest can promote widely accepted trends, there are also influencers and online communities that represent and promote specific niche or regional styles, creating micro-trends that can be equally influential in their specific contexts.

In conclusion, while fashion trends can reach global dissemination, they are far from being uniform worldwide. Fashion is a complex fabric of cultural expressions, practical needs, environmental influences, and individual creativity. This diversity not only enriches the world of fashion but also offers a window into the cultural and social nuances that characterize different regions of the world.

Cultural differences are a fundamental element in shaping the global fashion trend landscape. Each culture brings with it a unique set of aesthetics, values, and history that is reflected in fashion preferences. In Asia, for example, you may find a greater inclination towards styles that blend traditional elements with modernity, giving rise to a unique aesthetic that can be very different from what is popular in Europe or North America. In the latter, fashion may tend more towards individualism and experimentation, reflecting a different cultural and social context.

Color palettes, fabrics, and patterns used in a region can also be influenced by cultural factors. For example, in some Asian countries, vibrant colors and intricate patterns may be much more predominant compared to the more subdued tones and minimalist designs that you might find in some parts of Europe. These choices are not just a matter of taste but often have deep roots in the cultural history and art of a region.

In addition to cultural differences, climate and weather conditions play a significant role in shaping fashion trends. In countries with cold and harsh winters, for example, winter fashion may be characterized by heavy clothing, layering, and insulating fabrics. In contrast, in countries with warmer climates, fashion tends to focus on lightweight, airy designs and comfortable clothing that suits high temperatures. This diversity not only affects what is practical and comfortable but also what is perceived as fashionable or appropriate in a particular climate context.

Fashion brands, therefore, must carefully consider these variations when creating and distributing their collections in different parts of the world. A collection that succeeds in one country may not be equally popular in another due to differences in cultural tastes, climate, or other local preferences. Recognizing this diversity is crucial to fully understand the complexity and richness of the world of fashion.

In summary, while the fashion industry has a global reach, it is important to recognize that fashion trends are not uniform worldwide. Fashion is deeply influenced by a variety of cultural, social, economic, and environmental factors, leading to a diversity of styles and preferences in different regions. Recognizing this diversity is essential to fully understand the complexity and richness of the world of fashion.

COLOR AND PERSONALIZED ANALYSIS

Chromology, a fundamental concept in the field of personalized color analysis, plays a crucial role in the world of fashion and personal style. This discipline focuses on the theory that each person has a color palette that harmonizes perfectly with their unique physical characteristics, such as skin tone, eye color, and hair color. The goal of chromology is to identify this range of colors, ensuring that what we wear enhances our natural appearance.

Integrating chromology into the profession of image consulting or personal shopping means providing a more accurate and personalized service. Through the analysis of an individual's unique characteristics, professionals can recommend clothing, accessories, makeup, and even hair colors that harmonize with the client's natural palette. This approach not only enhances the aesthetic appearance but also contributes to creating a sense of harmony and coherence in the client's image.

Chromology is based on classifying people into different "seasons" based on their characteristics. For example, a person with warm undertones in their skin and golden hair might be classified as "autumn," implying that they look best in warm and earthy colors. In contrast, someone with cool undertones in their skin and black hair might be a "winter," suited for bright and cool colors.

In addition to choosing the right colors, chromology also considers the emotional and psychological impact of colors. Different colors evoke different reactions and emotions, both in the wearer and the observer. With a deep understanding of these principles, fashion professionals can guide their clients in selecting outfits for specific occasions where the psychological effect of color is as important as the aesthetic aspect.

Incorporating chromology into the work of a fashion professional is not just about matching the right colors; it is a way to help clients express their personality and enhance their image and self-esteem. Wearing colors that harmonize with one's natural features can significantly improve a person's aesthetic appearance and positively influence self-confidence. In this way, chromology becomes a fundamental element in creating a personal image that is not only aesthetically pleasing but also deeply in tune with the individual.

Here is some more detailed information about chromology. It is a color theory applied to personal image that is based on the idea, as mentioned earlier, that every individual can be associated with a specific "season" based on the natural color characteristics of their skin, eyes, and hair. This theory focuses on determining which colors suit a person best, with the goal of enhancing their natural beauty. Here's a more detailed explanation:

Fundamental Principles of Chromology:

Chromology is based on two main aspects of color: temperature (warm or cool) and intensity (light or dark, vibrant or subdued). These two factors help determine which colors look best on a person. The theory is based on the idea that people have an undertone of the skin that can be cool, neutral, or warm and that this undertone influences which colors appear more harmonious on them.

The Four Seasons of Chromology:

Traditionally, chromology classifies people into four groups, each associated with a "season": Spring, Summer, Autumn, and Winter. Each season is characterized by a specific range of colors:

- **Spring**: People with bright and warm characteristics. Ideal colors are vivid, bright, and warm, such as coral, cream, and gold.

- **Summer**: Soft and cool features. Recommended colors are cool, slightly muted, such as soft navy blue, pale pink, or lavender.

- **Autumn**: Rich and warm characteristics. Ideal colors include earthy and saturated shades, like burnt orange, olive green, and golden brown.

- **Winter**: Individuals with intense and cool features. Winter colors are cool and vibrant or very dark, like black, bright white, and cherry red.

How Chromology Analysis Works:

A professional chromology analysis usually takes place with the assistance of an image consultant or color expert. During the session, various fabric shades are used to observe how different colors interact with the client's natural skin, eye, and hair color. The goal is to identify the client's season and, consequently, their ideal color palette.

Application of Chromology:

Once a person's season is determined, chromology can be used to choose not only clothing and accessories but also makeup, hair colors, and jewelry. The idea is to create a consistent and harmonious appearance that enhances the individual's natural beauty.

In conclusion, chromology is a powerful tool for enhancing personal image. Understanding and using colors that naturally harmonize with one's physical characteristics can significantly increase visual impact and self-confidence. This approach to fashion and personal style allows for more informed and personalized choices, emphasizing the unique beauty of each individual.

THE IMPORTANCE OF COLOR IN CLOTHING

The importance of color in clothing plays a fundamental role not only in the realm of fashion but also in non-verbal communication and personal expression. The choice of colors in our clothing can profoundly influence how we perceive ourselves and how others perceive us. Here is a deeper exploration of the importance of color in clothing:

Non-Verbal Communication:

Color, as a fundamental element of non-verbal communication, exerts a significant influence on how we interact and are perceived in social contexts. Each shade carries a wealth of meanings and cultural associations, influencing not only our self-perception but also how others perceive us. The way we choose and combine colors in our clothing can, therefore, communicate subtle messages about our personality, mood, and even intentions.

Consider red, a color that immediately captures attention. Often associated with passion, energy, and even danger, red can be used to make a bold statement. A red dress or a red tie can not only draw attention but also convey a sense of confidence and audacity. On the other hand, blue is generally linked to tranquility, stability, and reliability. Wearing blue can communicate trustworthiness and professionalism, making it a popular choice in workplace settings.

Black, timeless and classic, is often associated with elegance and power. A black outfit can convey sophistication and authority, but also a sense of mystery. It's important to note that black can also evoke feelings of sadness or negativity in certain cultural contexts, demonstrating how the perception of colors can vary based on cultural backgrounds.

Colors can also influence the dynamics of social interactions. For instance, vibrant colors like orange or yellow can convey optimism and openness, potentially making the individual more approachable and friendly in the eyes of others. On the contrary, softer or neutral colors can communicate a more reserved or professional approach.

Furthermore, color choice can reflect or influence emotional states. Wearing colors that make us feel comfortable can boost self-confidence and, consequently, how we interact with others. Conversely, wearing a color that doesn't align with our mood or personality can create dissonance, negatively impacting our self-perception and interaction with others.

In conclusion, color in clothing is a powerful tool of non-verbal communication, with the ability to influence perception and interaction. Awareness of how colors can convey subtle messages can significantly enhance how we present ourselves and interact with the world around us, making color choice not just a matter of personal style but also an important aspect of expression and non-verbal communication.

Psychological Effect:

The psychological effect of colors in clothing is deeply rooted in the human experience, influencing not only how we see ourselves but also how we feel. The choice of colors we wear each day can be a powerful means to influence our mood and self-perception, thus directly impacting our emotional well-being and confidence.

When we wear colors that we love and feel particularly suited to, it can work as a confidence booster. Like a personal armor, the right colors can give us that extra push needed to face the day with more confidence. For example, an outfit in a color that makes us feel radiant and lively can actually increase our sense of energy and optimism. This phenomenon, known as "enclothed cognition," highlights how our clothing can influence our mental state and even our behavior.

On the other hand, wearing colors that don't align with our mood or that we feel don't represent us adequately can create a kind of dissonance. If the color of a garment makes us feel uncomfortable or inadequate, it can reflect in decreased self-confidence and a general sense of discontent. For instance, wearing a color imposed by fashion trends but not reflecting our personality can make us feel like we're wearing a costume rather than expressing our true selves.

Moreover, colors can play a significant role in reflecting or even altering our mood. Warm and vibrant shades can inject a sense of joy and vitality, while cooler and subdued colors can induce a sense of calm and professionalism. This ability of colors to evoke specific emotions can be strategically used in our clothing choices to influence how we want to feel in certain situations.

This understanding of the psychological effect of colors offers valuable insight when it comes to choosing our clothing. It's not just about selecting colors we aesthetically like but also about choosing those that resonate with our inner mood, personality, and emotional needs. Consciously harnessing the power of colors can become an effective way to enhance our daily life, boosting self-confidence and emotional well-being through the choices we make in our wardrobe.

Highlighting Physical Features:

The role of colors in clothing in enhancing physical features is a fundamental aspect that goes beyond mere aesthetics. The right choice of colors can have a significantly positive effect on how our natural features are perceived, accentuating the unique beauty of each individual.

When it comes to highlighting features such as eye color, hair color, or skin tone, the strategic use of color can make a big difference. For instance, wearing a shade that contrasts with the color of our eyes can make them stand out strikingly. Someone with green eyes, for example, might wear a purple or red garment to accentuate the green. Similarly, colors that are on the opposite side of the color wheel from eye color can create a contrast that draws attention to the eyes.

Concerning skin tone, the right colors can make it appear brighter and more vibrant, while the wrong ones can make it seem dull or unnatural. People with warm undertones in their skin may find warm colors like red, orange, or yellow flattering, as they enhance the warmth of their skin. Conversely, cool colors like blue, green, or purple can be particularly flattering for those with cool skin undertones.

Hair color also plays a significant role in the choice of clothing colors. For example, blond hair can be accentuated by dark colors that create a strong contrast, while dark hair can be complemented by light or vibrant colors that illuminate the face.

Additionally, color choice can also help balance or emphasize certain body parts. Dark and neutral colors can be used to minimize areas one prefers not to emphasize, while bright colors and patterns can be used to draw attention to areas of the body one wishes to highlight.

In conclusion, smart and conscious use of colors in clothing can become a powerful tool to enhance the unique physical characteristics of a person. Understanding which colors work best with our natural features not only helps us look our best but also feel more confident and comfortable in our appearance.

Adaptability and Versatility:

The adaptability and versatility of colors in clothing are essential aspects in creating a functional and expressive wardrobe. Choosing the right colors can greatly influence how easily garments can be combined, offering a wider range of stylistic options and maximizing the use of each individual piece.

Neutral colors like black, white, gray, and beige are key elements for a versatile wardrobe. These colors serve as a solid foundation for countless combinations and are particularly useful for creating outfits suitable for various occasions. Their neutrality makes them easily matchable with any other color, allowing you to mix and match different pieces without the fear of color clashes. For example, a pair of black pants or a beige skirt can easily be paired with shirts, sweaters, or jackets of any color, making these items extremely functional and indispensable.

At the same time, introducing vibrant or unusual colors into your wardrobe can be an excellent way to add a personal touch and stand out. Colors like deep red, cobalt blue, or emerald green can transform an outfit from simple to extraordinary, adding vibrancy and showcasing a bold and confident personality. These colors can be used as accents in an otherwise neutral outfit or combined more boldly to create a truly unique and personal look.

However, it's important to consider balance and overall harmony when playing with vibrant or unusual colors. While they can add dynamism to an outfit, excessive use or combining many vibrant colors can result in overwhelming or disharmonious looks. The key is to find the right balance between personal expression and aesthetic coherence.

Additionally, strategic use of colors can help create the illusion of a larger wardrobe. By varying colored accessories such as scarves, jewelry, or bags, you can create different outfits starting from the same neutral base. This approach is not only economical but also sustainable, as it reduces the need to own a large number of different garments.

In conclusion, color choice in your wardrobe is a fundamental aspect of adaptability and versatility in personal style. While neutral colors offer a solid and easily matchable base, vibrant and unusual colors can infuse energy and originality. Understanding and experimenting with these two aspects of color can significantly expand the available stylistic options and help create a wardrobe that is both practical and an expression of your individuality.

Seasonality and Occasion:

Seasonality and appropriateness for the occasion are crucial aspects in choosing colors in clothing, reflecting not only current trends but also the ability to adapt to different social and environmental contexts. Selecting colors based on the season or specific event can greatly enrich the dressing experience, making clothing not only an expression of personal style but also a reflection of awareness and sensitivity to circumstances.

During different seasons, the colors we choose to wear often reflect changes in the natural environment and our mood. In spring and summer, colors tend to become brighter and lighter, reflecting the brightness and energy of these times of the year. Shades like lemon yellow, sky blue, or coral can evoke the vivacity of blooming nature and the carefree atmosphere of summer days. These colors not only add a touch of joy to the wardrobe but can also positively influence the mood, bringing a sense of joy and lightness.

Conversely, in autumn and winter, the color palette tends to shift towards darker and deeper tones. Colors like burgundy, forest green, or navy blue can evoke the richness and warmth needed in these colder months. These shades are not only practical for the cold seasons but also add a sense of elegance and depth to the clothing.

In addition to seasonality, colors play a fundamental role in occasion-appropriateness. In formal settings such as business meetings, ceremonies, or elegant events, neutral or dark colors like black, charcoal gray, or navy blue are often safe choices that convey professionalism and elegance. These colors are versatile and can be easily combined to create a refined and composed appearance.

For less formal occasions or leisure time, there is greater freedom in choosing colors. Here, you can experiment with bolder shades or play with color combinations to reflect a more relaxed and creative personal style. The use of vibrant or unusual colors can be a way to express your personality and stand out in an informal context.

In summary, considering seasonality and occasion in your choice of clothing colors not only ensures that you are dressed appropriately but also allows you to experiment and play with different color palettes. This approach allows you to create outfits that are not only aesthetically pleasing but also reflect an awareness of the context and situation, enriching the experience of expressing yourself through your style.

Expression of Identity and Culture:

Color in clothing is a powerful vehicle for expressing identity and culture, going beyond mere aesthetic preference. The choice of colors we wear can be a deep personal statement, a reflection of our personality, values, cultural roots, and life experiences. This dimension of colorful clothing allows us to communicate aspects of our inner selves without the need for words, establishing a direct connection between who we are and how we choose to present ourselves to the world.

For many people, the colors chosen for clothing can be a way to express individuality and uniqueness. Bold and vibrant colors can be a sign of an extroverted and creative personality, while more subdued and neutral tones can indicate a more introspective or minimalist nature. For example, someone who identifies with tranquility and harmony may prefer pastel shades, while an individual who loves to express energy and passion may opt for stronger and bolder hues.

Beyond personal expression, color in clothing can also serve as a powerful cultural symbol. In many cultures, specific colors have deeply rooted meanings and can be used to celebrate traditions, holidays, or rites of passage. These colors can serve as links to cultural heritage, reminding and honoring the roots and stories of a community. For example, red in many Asian cultures is considered an auspicious color and is often worn during celebrations, while in some African cultures, specific color schemes and patterns can indicate membership in a particular ethnic or regional group.

Additionally, colors can be used to make political or social statements. For example, adopting specific colors on certain occasions, such as wearing black to protest or pink to support gender-related issues, can be a way to express solidarity or support for a cause.

Therefore, color in clothing is a rich and complex means of expression that allows people to communicate who they are, where they come from, and what they believe in. This chromatic expression of identity and culture not only enriches an individual's wardrobe but also contributes to weaving the broader fabric of diversity and human expression. Through the choice of colors, we can celebrate our individuality, honor our cultural roots, and communicate our beliefs, contributing to a more colorful and diverse representation of the world we live in.

In conclusion, color in clothing is much more than a simple aesthetic choice; it is an expressive medium that has the power to influence perception, personal expression, and even social interaction. Awareness and thoughtful consideration in choosing colors can greatly enrich the dressing experience and help create an image that is authentic and reflective of individual personality.

CONCEPTS AND APPLICATIONS OF COLOR ANALYSIS

Color analysis is a method used to determine the colors that best suit an individual based on their unique physical characteristics and personal style. This approach goes beyond simply identifying an individual's favorite colors; it considers how specific shades can enhance or diminish a person's natural beauty. Here is a deeper exploration of the concepts and applications of color analysis:

Fundamental Concepts of Color Analysis:

Color analysis is based on principles of harmony and contrast. Elements such as skin tone (warm or cool), eye color, and hair color are considered to determine which color palettes harmonize best with a person's natural features. This process helps identify colors that enhance overall appearance, making the skin appear brighter, eyes more vibrant, and hair more lively.

Color Analysis Methodology:

Color analysis often involves the use of colored drapes or fabrics in various shades, placed near the person's face to observe the chromatic effects on the skin, eyes, and hair. This technique helps determine which colors best accentuate natural features and which ones may make them appear dull or less attractive.

Applications in Clothing and Style:

Once the ideal color palette is determined, it can be applied to clothing, accessories, and even makeup. Choosing garments and accessories in the right colors can transform an outfit, highlighting an individual's strengths and creating an overall more harmonious and balanced look.

Benefits of Color Analysis:

Using colors that complement one's physical characteristics can have a significant impact on self-confidence and self-esteem. Wearing colors that enhance one's appearance can make individuals feel more attractive, confident, and comfortable in their style. Additionally, it can simplify clothing choices and shopping, as there is a clear guide on which colors to look for.

Extension Beyond Clothing:

Color analysis can also be applied in contexts beyond clothing. For example, it can be useful in choosing makeup colors, home decor, or even personal and professional branding.

Personalization and Flexibility:

Although color analysis provides guidelines, it's essential to remember that it is a flexible tool. Personal preferences, occasions, and trends can influence style choices, allowing individuals to play with the recommended palette and adapt it to their needs.

In conclusion, color analysis is a valuable practice that can significantly enrich the experience of dressing and expressing oneself through style. By providing guidance on which colors best suit an individual, it can enhance visual impact and self-confidence, enabling the creation of a personal image that is not only aesthetically pleasing but also deeply in tune with the individual.

FREQUENTLY ASKED QUESTIONS: HOW TO CHOOSE THE RIGHT COLORS FOR ME?

Choosing the right colors for clothing is a topic that raises many questions, as it involves both the aesthetic and functional aspects of dressing. Here are some of the most frequently asked questions on the subject:

How Can I Determine Which Colors Suit Me Best?

To discover which colors enhance your appearance, consider the color of your hair, eyes, and the undertone of your skin. Warm skin undertones tend to be complemented by warm colors like red, orange, and yellow, while cool undertones go well with cool colors like blue, green, and purple. There are various tests to determine skin undertone, including observing the color of the veins on your wrist.

Are There Universal Colors That Look Good on Everyone?

Some colors, known as "universal," tend to look good on many people regardless of their skin undertone. Examples include certain shades of blue (like denim blue), some grays, and bottle green.

How Can I Choose Colors for a Versatile Wardrobe?

For a versatile wardrobe, it's recommended to have a base of neutral colors such as black, white, gray, beige, and navy. These colors can easily be paired with a variety of other colors and patterns, making it easier to create different outfits.

Can I Wear Colors That Are Not in My Ideal Palette?

Certainly! While color analysis can provide useful guidelines, you're not limited to them exclusively. Experimenting with colors can be a fun way to express your personality. The key is to feel comfortable and confident in what you're wearing.

How Can I Use Colors to Influence My Mood?

Colors can have a significant impact on your mood. For example, vibrant colors like yellow or red can increase energy and vitality, while pastel tones can have a calming effect. Choose the colors of your outfit based on how you want to feel or the message you want to convey on that day.

Can the Colors I Wear Affect How Others Perceive Me?

Yes, colors can influence how others perceive you. For instance, wearing dark and solid colors can convey a sense of authority and professionalism, while light and soft colors can give an impression of approachability and kindness.

In summary, choosing the right colors for clothing depends on a combination of personal factors, such as skin undertone, hair and eye color, and personal preferences. While there are guidelines based on color analysis, it's essential to remember that personal expression and comfort with your clothing choices are equally important.

DEBUNKING MYTHS: SOME COLORS DON'T LOOK GOOD ON ANYONE

The myth that some colors don't look good on anyone is a widespread belief, but in reality, it is an oversimplification that fails to consider the variety and complexity of individual characteristics and personal preferences. This idea overly simplifies the concept of color coordination and does not reflect the reality that almost every color can be successfully worn by someone, depending on how it is paired and the context in which it is worn. Here's why this myth is unfounded:

Individual Variations:

Each person has a unique set of physical characteristics, such as skin tone, eye color, and hair color, which can be enhanced or diminished by different colors. What may not look good on one person could be extremely flattering to another. For example, a color that may appear dull on cool-toned skin could illuminate warm-toned skin.

Context and Pairing:

The key to wearing any color successfully lies in context and pairing. A color that may not be particularly flattering on its own can be transformed when correctly combined with other colors or specific accessories. The combination of colors and the choice of accessories can drastically change the visual impact of a clothing item.

Personal Preferences and Style:

Color choice is also a matter of personal taste and individual style.

Even if a color is not traditionally considered flattering, it can still be a style choice for someone who appreciates it and feels comfortable wearing it. Fashion is a form of personal expression, and choosing colors that one loves and feels comfortable in is more important than adhering to rigid rules.

Changes in Fashion Trends:

Fashion trends are constantly evolving, and what was once considered a "no-go" in terms of color can suddenly become fashionable. The fashion industry often redefines which colors are desirable or not, demonstrating that there are no universally unsuitable colors.

In conclusion, the myth that certain colors don't look good on anyone should be debunked. The choice of colors in clothing should be based on a variety of factors, including compatibility with individual characteristics, personal preferences, the context in which the color is worn, and the skill of combining and balancing different colors. Almost all colors can be suitable for someone, and the beauty of wearing them lies in the art of knowing how and when to do so.

CLOTHING AND MALE/FEMALE ACCESSORIES

In the chapter dedicated to both male and female clothing and accessories, we delve into the vast and fascinating world of fashion, where style, functionality, and personal expression intersect to create the image we project to the world. This sartorial universe is not just a collection of trends and fashionable garments; it represents an ongoing dialogue between our identity and how we choose to present ourselves to others.

Clothing and accessories, essential elements of this dialogue, go beyond the mere necessity of getting dressed. They are tools of self-expression, means through which we can convey our personality, mood, and even our goals. In this context, we explore how fashion choices can influence how others perceive us and how we can use clothing and accessories to emphasize our strengths and show the world who we truly are.

In an ever-evolving landscape where trends come and go at astonishing speed, maintaining a personal style that is both up-to-date and true to one's essence may seem like a challenge. However, with targeted tips and guides on how to combine different clothing elements, it is possible to create a look that is contemporary yet unique. From coordinating colors and fabrics to choosing the right accessories, we will explore how small choices can have a significant impact on the overall look.

We will also address some common questions about refreshing one's personal style, offering practical advice and ideas for updating the wardrobe without losing sight of one's identity. Additionally, we will debunk the myth that accessories are less important than clothing. Accessories can indeed be the finishing touch that transforms an ordinary outfit into something extraordinary, underscoring the importance of every detail in building one's style.

This chapter aims to be a comprehensive guide to navigate the world of clothing and accessories, providing tools and knowledge to express oneself through fashion, regardless of gender. With a holistic approach to the world of dressing, we aim to explore how every element of our wardrobe can contribute to telling our story, celebrating the diversity and creativity that fashion can offer.

In the field of both men's and women's clothing and accessories, keeping up with the latest trends and knowing how to integrate them into your personal style can be both exciting and a bit intimidating. Fashion trends are constantly evolving, capturing the essence of a cultural moment, an artistic expression, or a shift in social preferences. In this section, we will explore some current trends and provide specific tips for adopting them in the most harmonious and personal way possible.

For men, a recent trend is the return of classic elements but with a modern twist. This can include the reuse of traditional items such as tailored jackets or chino pants, but reinterpreted in vibrant colors or with more relaxed cuts. The idea is to balance the classic with the innovative, creating a look that is respectful of tradition but at the same time fresh and current.

For women, a key trend is the bold use of patterns and colors. We are seeing an increase in bold prints, both in terms of size and color. These can range from geometric patterns to floral prints and can be used to create focal points in an outfit. Mixing different prints may seem risky, but when done carefully, it can result in a sophisticated and eclectic ensemble.

In both cases, the emphasis is on personalization and individual expression. Here are some tips for integrating these trends into your own style:

Balancing Old and New: When exploring new trends, it's important to strike a balance between fashion-forward elements and classic pieces. This helps create a look that is contemporary without being over-the-top.

Experimenting with Colors: Don't be afraid to experiment with colors. Even though bold prints and vibrant colors may seem intimidating, they can be incorporated in small doses, such as an accessory or a single garment, to add a touch of vibrancy to the outfit.

Mixing Fabrics and Textures: Playing with different fabrics and textures can add depth and interest to an outfit. For example, pairing smooth fabric with a rougher one or using layering can create a dynamic and intriguing look.

Accessories as Focal Points: Accessories are a great way to integrate new trends without overhauling your entire wardrobe. A trendy accessory can update an outfit without the need for a complete wardrobe makeover.

Confidence in Your Style: Lastly, the key to adopting any trend is to do so with confidence. Choose what resonates with you and what makes you feel comfortable and confident. Fashion is ultimately a way to express who you are, so every choice should be a reflection of your personality.

Through these tips, you can navigate the ever-changing world of fashion, incorporating new trends in a way that reflects your personal style and enriches the way you present yourself to the world.

Creating effective and harmonious clothing and accessory combinations is an essential component of dressing with style. Whether you're putting together an outfit for a formal event, work, or leisure, there are some principles and techniques that can help you build aesthetically pleasing and functional combinations. Below, we explore a detailed guide on how to match clothes and accessories effectively:

Understanding Color Balance:

Understanding color balance is a crucial element in the art of clothing pairing, as it is one of the determining factors in the visual impact of an outfit. A thorough understanding of how the color wheel works can help you create harmonious and eye-catching color combinations, as well as express your personal style more effectively.

The color wheel is a fundamental tool for understanding the relationships between different colors. It consists of primary colors (red, blue, and yellow), secondary colors (green, orange, and purple, obtained by mixing primaries), and tertiary colors (combinations of primaries and secondaries).

Complementary Colors:

Colors opposite each other on the color wheel, known as complementary colors, create a high contrast and are visually stimulating. This combination is often used to create a focal point or add a bold touch to an outfit. For example, pairing a blue shirt with orange accessories can create a vibrant and attractive contrast. However, it's important to use this combination in moderation to avoid overwhelming the look.

Analogous Colors:

For a more subdued and harmonious approach, analogous color combinations are ideal. These colors are found next to each other on the color wheel and usually share a common undertone, whether warm or cool. For example, a combination of various shades of blue and green can create a cohesive and tranquil look. This type of pairing is perfect for those who prefer a more understated but still stylistically cohesive appearance.

Variations in Saturation and Brightness:

In addition to color selection, it's important to consider saturation (color intensity) and brightness (how light or dark a color is). Playing with these two dimensions can add interest and depth to an outfit. For example, pairing a vibrant color with a darker or lighter version of itself can create a pleasing chromatic gradation.

Neutral Colors:

Neutral colors, such as black, white, gray, beige, and navy, provide an excellent foundation for any color scheme. They are versatile and can be easily paired with more vibrant colors to balance the outfit. For example, a pair of beige pants with an electric blue shirt can be an effective yet understated combination.

Experimentation and Personal Preferences:

There are no fixed rules in the world of color, so experimenting with different combinations is essential. Everyone reacts to colors differently, so it's important to find what works best for you and reflects your personality and style.

In summary, color balancing in clothing is a combination of art and science. Understanding how colors work together and how they influence visual perception will allow you to create outfits that are not only aesthetically pleasing but also expressions of your personal style. Remember that fashion is a field where you can express yourself, so don't be afraid to play and experiment with colors.

Playing with Texture and Materials:

The art of playing with texture and materials in clothing is a subtle dance of balance and contrast that can elevate an outfit from ordinary to extraordinary. Combining different fabrics not only adds visual and tactile variety to a look but also allows for creative expression and uniqueness in dressing. Here's how you can make the most of the variety of textures and materials available:

Contrasting between Soft and Rough:

Creating a contrast between soft and rough elements can add an interesting dimension to an outfit. For example, pairing a soft cashmere sweater with rough tweed pants or a denim jacket can create a visually pleasing balance. This type of contrast not only captures attention but also adds a level of complexity to your style.

Mixing Heavy and Light:

Combining heavy fabrics with lighter materials is another effective technique. For instance, a heavy wool coat over a light chiffon dress can create a layered look that works well in transitional seasons. This combination is not only functional but also adds depth and movement to the outfit.

Combining Smooth and Textured:

Playing with texture can also mean experimenting with smooth surfaces against textured ones. One example could be pairing a smooth silk top with corduroy pants or a jacquard fabric skirt. The difference in textures can make the outfit more dynamic and visually stimulating.

Using Glossy and Matte Fabrics:

Pairing fabrics with different finishes, such as glossy and matte materials, can create a sophisticated effect. A shiny satin jacket paired with matte cotton or wool pants can create a contrast that catches the eye without being excessive.

Experimenting with Patterns and Prints:

In addition to textures, consider playing with patterns and prints. For example, a top with thin stripes can be paired with a polka-dot skirt for a playful look, or a plaid blazer can be matched with solid-color pants for a more understated look.

Careful Fabric Selection:

When experimenting with different fabrics, it's essential to consider the quality and drape of the materials. Some fabrics drape better than others and can significantly influence the overall look of the outfit. For instance, a fabric that drapes softly and fluidly can add a sense of elegance, while a stiffer fabric can provide structure and shape to the outfit.

Consistency in Occasion and Comfort:

While experimenting with textures and materials, always consider the occasion and your personal comfort. Ensure that the chosen fabrics are suitable for the context in which they will be worn, and that you feel comfortable and confident in your outfit.

In conclusion, playing with textures and materials offers endless possibilities to express your individuality through your style. This creative exploration not only enhances the aesthetic aspect of your clothing but also allows you to experiment and discover new ways to express yourself through fashion.

Balancing Basic Pieces and Statement Pieces:

The art of creating a balanced outfit that harmoniously mixes basic pieces and statement pieces is fundamental for clothing that is both interesting and measured. This balance allows you to play with fashion without going to extremes while maintaining a stylistic coherence that is both visually pleasing and expressive of your individuality.

Basic pieces, often in neutral colors like black, white, gray, beige, or navy, are the foundation of your wardrobe. They serve as a canvas on which to build the rest of the outfit. These items, such as a white shirt, well-tailored jeans, or a black blazer, are versatile and timeless, offering a solid base for experimenting with bolder pieces.

Statement pieces, on the other hand, are the ones that capture attention. They can be colorful, with vibrant patterns, unconventional cuts, or adorned with unique details. These elements are an expression of your personality and creativity. However, it's essential not to overdo it. The goal is to attract attention positively without overwhelming visually.

When creating an outfit, the idea is to choose a statement piece as the focal point and build the rest of the outfit around it with basic pieces. For example, if you choose to wear a skirt with a colorful and bold pattern, you might balance it with a simple top in a neutral color and a pair of understated shoes. This allows the skirt to be the center of attention without making the outfit too complicated or chaotic.

Another approach is to pair several statement pieces cautiously. For instance, if you wear a printed shirt, you could match it with pants in a color found in the print. This creates a visual connection between the two pieces, maintaining the overall harmony of the outfit.

Additionally, it's important to consider the context and the occasion. While a more creative or casual environment may allow for more freedom in mixing statement pieces, in a formal or professional setting, it might be more appropriate to limit the use of such pieces and opt for a more restrained and refined look.

Finally, remember that fashion is a way to express yourself. Don't be afraid to experiment and find your personal balance between basic and statement pieces. The goal is to feel confident and comfortable in what you wear, creating a style that reflects who you are.

Considering Silhouette and Fit:

Considering the silhouette and fit is crucial in the art of clothing pairing, as the shape and fit of garments can significantly influence the overall look and impression that an outfit conveys. Understanding how to flatter your figure through the choice of the right clothing is a key skill in creating a look that is not only aesthetically pleasing but also expressive and comfortable.

Enhancing Figure:

Every person has a unique body shape, and understanding how to enhance it can make a difference in how an outfit appears.

Clothes that follow the body's natural line without being too tight or restrictive tend to be more flattering. For example, for those with an hourglass figure, clothes that highlight the waist can accentuate their natural silhouette.

Balancing Proportions:

Balancing proportions is a crucial aspect of pairing. If you wear a loose or voluminous garment in one part of your body, balance it with something more fitted in another. For example, a wide or flared skirt can be balanced with a fitted top or a tucked-in blouse, creating a visual balance that doesn't weigh down the figure.

Choosing Fabrics and Drape:

The choice of fabrics and their drape plays a significant role in the silhouette a garment creates. More fluid and lightweight materials can drape gracefully, emphasizing curves subtly, while stiffer fabrics can provide structure and shape. For example, a chiffon dress can drape softly around the body, while a thicker fabric can create a more defined silhouette.

Attention to Fit:

Fit, or how well a garment fits, is crucial to ensure that clothes are comfortable and enhance your figure. Clothes that are too tight or too loose can distort the perception of your body's proportions. It's essential to choose clothes that fit well, respecting the body's natural shape without constraining it.

Using Accessories to Modify Silhouette:

Accessories can be used to visually modify the silhouette. A belt, for example, can be used to define the waist, while a long scarf can add verticality and elongate the figure. Even the choice of shoes can influence the perception of the silhouette; high heels, for instance, can lengthen the figure.

Adaptability to Personal Style:

While considering these aspects, it's also crucial that the clothing reflects your personal style. You don't need to rigidly adhere to fixed rules if they don't align with your aesthetic sense or what makes you feel comfortable.

In conclusion, considering the silhouette and fit is vital in assembling outfits that not only appear well-put-together but also enhance your unique features. A well-thought-out pairing that takes into account body shape and fit can boost self-confidence and ensure that you feel your best in what you wear.

Using Accessories to Complete or Break Monotony:

Accessories can transform an outfit. A colorful scarf or a statement necklace can add a point of interest to an otherwise simple attire. Similarly, a belt can be used to define the silhouette or add a touch of color.

Matching Shoes and Bags:

In the art of clothing pairing, the choice of shoes and bags can play a crucial role in the overall harmony of an outfit. Although an exact color match between shoes and bags is no longer a strict rule in contemporary fashion, it's still essential for these two elements to complement each other, creating a cohesive and polished look.

Complementarity between shoes and bags can be achieved through various techniques. For example, matching texture rather than the exact color can be an effective way to create harmony. A brown leather bag, with its rich and natural texture, can be charmingly paired with shoes in earthy tones like beige, camel, or even a darker brown, creating a combination that is both subtle and aesthetically pleasing.

Another approach might be to play with chromatic contrasts in a balanced way. For instance, a bag in a bright color like red or blue can be paired with shoes in a neutral shade that contains a hint of that color. This type of pairing creates an interesting focal point without making the outfit too heavy or dissonant.

You can also experiment with combinations based on seasonal trends or color themes. For example, during autumn, warmer and earthy color combinations can be particularly effective, while in spring and summer, brighter and lighter colors can be a fresh and fashionable choice.

In addition to color and texture, the shape and style of shoes and bags can also contribute to the overall consistency of the outfit. A sleek and structured bag, for example, might pair well with shoes with a refined and formal design, while a casual and slouchy bag can complement more relaxed and comfortable shoes.

Moreover, it's essential to consider the occasion and the context in which they will be worn. For a formal event, it's advisable to go for a more classic and refined pairing, while for daily or casual activities, you can be more experimental and playful in your choices.

In conclusion, matching shoes and bags doesn't necessarily have to follow rigid rules, but it should aim to create a sense of balance and harmony in the overall outfit. This can be achieved through complementarity in color, texture, shape, and style, always keeping the occasion and context in mind. A well-executed pairing not only enhances the overall appearance but also adds a touch of sophistication and attention to detail, which are key elements of good style.

Layering and Seasonality:

The combination of different layers, or layering, is an essential technique in fashion, especially to adapt to various seasons while maintaining a sense of style. This practice not only provides versatility and functionality but also offers the opportunity to play with different combinations of fabrics, colors, and shapes, creating unique and personalized outfits.

During the colder months, layering becomes particularly important. Starting with a lightweight base, such as a shirt or a T-shirt, you can then add intermediate layers like sweaters, cardigans, or vests. These layers not only provide additional warmth but also add depth and visual interest to the outfit. For the finishing touch, a well-chosen coat or jacket can complete the look, providing not only extra protection from the elements but also a distinctive style element.

In layering, it's essential to consider the balance of volumes and lengths. Pairing a loose or bulky garment with more fitted ones can help maintain a balanced silhouette. For example, if you wear an oversized sweater, you might balance it with snug-fitting pants or a narrow skirt. Similarly, layering pieces of different lengths can create a visually interesting layered effect, such as a long cardigan over a shorter top, finished with a knee-length coat.

It's also crucial to consider colors and patterns when creating layers. While one layer may have a bold color or pattern, the other layers could be more neutral to avoid making the outfit too chaotic. For example, a vibrant printed scarf can be the perfect accent on a coat in neutral tones and a simple sweater.

In spring and summer, layering remains a useful technique, although with a slightly different approach. Instead of layering for warmth, it's more about layering for style and versatility. Lightweight vests, kimonos, thin cardigans, or lightweight jackets can be used to add interest to an outfit without suffocating. In these cases, layering allows for easy adaptation to temperature changes during the day.

In conclusion, layering is a versatile style technique that can be adapted to any season and occasion. Experimenting with different layers, textures, colors, and lengths not only allows you to stay comfortable and temperature-appropriate but also offers a unique opportunity to express your creativity and sense of style. With a bit of practice, you can master the art of layering to create outfits that are both functional and aesthetically pleasing.

Adaptability and Versatility:

Adaptability and versatility are key concepts in the world of fashion, especially when it comes to creating a functional and stylistically consistent wardrobe. The ability to mix and match pieces in different ways not only extends the range of available outfit options but also maximizes the use of each clothing item, offering both economic and environmental sustainability. When selecting and pairing garments, it's crucial to consider how each element can be reused and reinvented in various contexts.

Multifunctional Pieces:

Investing in multifunctional pieces that can be worn in multiple ways or on different occasions is a smart strategy. For example, a high-quality shirt can be worn under a sweater for a casual look, with a blazer for a more formal context, or even on its own with a pair of jeans for everyday wear. This versatility makes the garment valuable in terms of variety of use.

Cross-Matching:

When choosing clothes, think about how each piece could be paired with various others in your wardrobe. Items in neutral colors or easily combinable tones offer a wide range of options and can be creatively combined with brighter colors or unique patterns. For example, a pair of black pants is a classic that can be paired with almost anything, from a formal shirt to a graphic T-shirt.

Transitioning Between Seasons:

Select clothing that can be easily adapted to changing seasons. For example, a lightweight dress can be worn alone in summer and then layered with sweaters, tights, and boots in winter. This ability to adapt to different temperatures and weather conditions extends the lifespan of the garment throughout the year.

Accessories for Refreshing:

Accessories play a crucial role in adding variety to an outfit. Changing accessories like shoes, bags, jewelry, belts, or scarves can completely transform the look of a basic garment. This allows you to create different outfits without necessarily investing in new clothing items.

Strategic Layering:

Experimenting with layering can offer new ways to wear existing pieces. By layering different items, you can create fresh combinations and adapt clothing to various temperatures and occasions.

Customization and Adaptation:

Don't hesitate to personalize or modify garments to increase their versatility. Small adjustments, such as changing buttons, shortening or lengthening hems, or adding decorative details, can breathe new life into an old or simple piece.

In summary, the key to an adaptable and versatile wardrobe lies in selecting pieces that offer a variety of styling options and can be easily transformed or combined in different ways. This approach not only makes personal style more dynamic and interesting but also promotes more conscious and sustainable fashion consumption.

Personal Expression:

Finally, the most important thing in pairing is that it reflects your personality and unique style. Don't hesitate to break the "rules" if it means better expressing who you are. Fashion is a space for exploration and self-expression, so experiment and find what works for you.

Through these principles and techniques, you can learn to create pairings that not only look aesthetically pleasing but also reflect your personal identity. Remember that the goal is not only to follow trends but also to find ways to express yourself through the choices you make in your clothing.

FREQUENTLY ASKED QUESTIONS: HOW CAN I UPDATE MY STYLE?

Updating your style is a common question among those who want to refresh their image or simply keep up with the evolution of fashion. There are several ways to refresh your style without necessarily overhauling your entire wardrobe. Here are some effective strategies:

Incorporate Current Trends:

One of the simplest ways to update your style is to incorporate some current trends. This doesn't mean blindly following every new fashion trend, but rather selecting a few pieces or accessories that resonate with your personal style and can be easily paired with the items you already own.

Revisit Classics:

Sometimes, updating your style can mean going back to classics. Timeless pieces like a well-tailored jacket, a quality pair of jeans, or a white shirt can be brought back into fashion with minor adjustments or modern accessories.

Play with Accessories:

Accessories are an effective way to add a touch of freshness to your look. Scarves, jewelry, watches, belts, or bags can transform an outfit and are a cost-effective way to experiment with the latest trends.

Experiment with Colors and Patterns:

By introducing new colors or patterns into your wardrobe, you can refresh your look. This could mean adding pieces in vibrant colors that aren't normally part of your palette or experimenting with different prints and textures.

Modify Fit and Silhouette:

Sometimes, all it takes to update your style is a change in the silhouette or fit of your clothes. Try wearing garments with a different fit from what you usually choose, such as switching from fitted clothing to looser and more fluid cuts, or vice versa.

Add Trendy Pieces:

Purchasing a few key trendy pieces can give an immediate freshness to your look. It could be a clothing item, like a jacket in a particular color or cut, or an accessory like a stylish pair of shoes or a trendy bag.

Recycle and Revamp:

Don't underestimate the power of recycling and revamping. Adapting or customizing the clothing you already own can not only be a creative activity but also a way to create a unique look that reflects your personal style.

Seek Inspiration:

Find inspiration by looking at fashion blogs, magazines, style influencers, or even people in real life. Sometimes, all it takes to update your style is a new perspective or a fresh idea on how to combine items in ways you hadn't considered.

Remember, updating your style doesn't necessarily mean having to follow every new fashion trend. It's about finding ways to express your personality and unique taste while keeping your look fresh and current.

MYTHS TO DEBUNK: ACCESSORIES ARE LESS IMPORTANT THAN CLOTHING

The myth that accessories are less important than clothing is a limiting notion that underestimates the potential impact accessories can have on an outfit. Accessories, in fact, play a crucial role in completing, defining, and enriching a look, and in many cases, they can completely transform the overall appearance of an outfit. Here's why it's important to debunk this myth:

Style Definition:

Accessories are often what sets apart a common outfit from an exceptional one. They can reflect your personality and unique style in ways that clothing alone may not achieve. A simple black dress can be transformed into an evening look with the addition of elegant jewelry or made suitable for a casual setting with a colorful scarf and a pair of sneakers.

Flexibility and Versatility:

Accessories provide a way to refresh your wardrobe without the need to buy new clothes. By changing accessories, you can breathe new life into garments you've worn many times, making them suitable for different occasions and seasons. A change of bag, shoes, or hat can radically alter the look of an outfit.

Personal Expression and Creativity:

Accessories allow for creativity and personal expression. They can be a way to showcase your interests, such as a vintage brooch for antique enthusiasts or a designer watch for horology enthusiasts. They are also a way to play with colors, shapes, and textures that might be more challenging to incorporate into main clothing pieces.

Balance and Proportion:

Accessories can help balance body proportions. For example, a belt can be used to define the waist, glasses can balance the face shape, and pointed shoes can elongate the legs. These small adjustments can have a significant impact on the overall appearance of the outfit.

Adaptability to Trends and Seasons:

Accessories are a cost-effective way to keep up with current trends. Instead of overhauling your entire wardrobe every season, adding a few trendy accessories can be a more sustainable and practical way to stay fashionable.

In conclusion, accessories are essential elements in the world of fashion and personal styling. They are versatile tools that offer endless possibilities for personalizing and refreshing a look, demonstrating that they can be just as important, if not more so, than the clothing itself. So, when you think about your outfit, consider accessories as key components that can define and elevate your style.

FABRIC ANALYSIS PART 1 AND 2

In the journey through the world of fashion and personal style, a fundamental chapter is dedicated to fabric analysis. This part of the book, divided into two sections, provides a comprehensive and detailed overview of fabrics, exploring their variety, unique characteristics, and the impact they can have on creating an outfit. Fabrics are much more than mere materials from which clothes are made; they are the canvas on which the art of fashion is painted, influencing everything from silhouette and comfort to how a garment adapts to different situations and climates.

The first section of this chapter focuses on types and properties of fabrics. Here, we will explore the wide range of materials available, from natural fibers like cotton, wool, and silk to synthetic fibers like polyester and nylon. Each fabric has distinctive characteristics in terms of texture, weight, durability, and how it drapes and conforms to the body. Understanding these properties is essential for making informed choices when it comes to selecting clothing, both for everyday life and special occasions.

In the second section, we will delve into choosing the right fabric based on specific occasions and body types. This part is dedicated to guiding the reader in selecting fabrics that not only suit the style and event but also flatter the body's shape, enhancing the overall look of the outfit. Whether it's finding the perfect material for an elegant evening gown or comfortable leisurewear, choosing the right fabric is crucial to ensure that the garment is not only visually pleasing but also comfortable to wear.

Through these sections, the reader will gain in-depth knowledge of different fabrics, learning to recognize their quality, functionality, and compatibility with various lifestyles and weather conditions. This understanding will enable making more conscious and sustainable choices, elevating the dressing experience to a higher level, where every fabric choice is a mindful step toward creating a look that not only looks extraordinary but also feels equally special.

TYPES AND PROPERTIES OF FABRICS

The section on the types and properties of fabrics represents an essential part in understanding clothing and fashion. Each fabric possesses unique characteristics that influence not only the appearance and functionality of a garment but also how it is perceived and experienced by the wearer. Here is a detailed overview of various types of fabrics and their distinctive properties:

Cotton:

Cotton is a natural fiber known for its versatility, comfort, and breathability. It absorbs moisture, making it ideal for summer clothing and garments in direct contact with the skin. However, it tends to wrinkle easily and may shrink if not properly treated.

Wool:

Wool is a natural fiber primarily obtained from sheep. It is valued for its insulating properties and its ability to regulate temperature. Wool can be lightweight or heavy, depending on the weave, and is ideal for winter garments. However, it requires careful care to maintain its shape and quality.

Silk:

Silk, known for its luxurious appearance and softness, is a natural fiber produced by silkworms. It is lightweight and has a beautiful sheen, making it popular for eveningwear and scarves. However, it is delicate and can be damaged by sunlight and sweat.

Linen:

Linen, derived from flax plants, is appreciated for its strength and freshness. It is particularly suitable for summer clothing due to its excellent breathability. However, it tends to wrinkle easily.

Polyester:

Polyester is a synthetic fiber that is strong, durable, and easy to care for. It does not wrinkle easily and retains color well, but it is not as breathable as natural fibers, which can make it less comfortable in hot climates.

Rayon/Viscose:

Rayon or viscose is a man-made fiber created from natural materials like cellulose. It is soft and has a lovely draped appearance but can shrink or distort when wet.

Nylon:

Nylon is a synthetic fiber known for its strength and durability. It is often used in activewear and stockings due to its flexibility and resistance to wear. However, it is not very breathable.

Denim:

Denim, traditionally made from cotton, is a sturdy fabric primarily used for jeans and jackets. It has good durability and tends to improve with age but can be stiff and heavy.

Cashmere:

Cashmere, derived from the hair of cashmere goats, is known for its incredible softness and thermal insulation. It is luxurious and lightweight but requires careful care and can be expensive.

Velvet:

A richly textured fabric known for its softness and luxurious appearance. It is often used in formal clothing and eveningwear.

Tweed:

A robust wool fabric with a distinctive texture. It is popular for jackets and outerwear, especially in casual and country settings.

Chiffon:

A lightweight and sheer fabric, often made of silk or polyester. It is used for elegant dresses and flowing garments due to its lightness and beautiful draping effect.

Gabardine:

A sturdy and tightly woven fabric, typically in wool or cotton, used for coats and suits. It is known for its durability and weather resistance.

Lace:

A decorative fabric that creates intricate and detailed patterns. It is widely used in formal clothing, wedding dresses, and lingerie.

Tencel/Lyocell:

An artificial fiber made from cellulose, known for its softness, strength, and sustainability. It is a popular eco-friendly alternative for various types of clothing.

Spandex/Elastane:

A synthetic fiber known for its exceptional elasticity. It is often blended with other fabrics to add stretch to jeans, activewear, and lingerie.

Organza:

A thin and transparent fabric, often in silk, characterized by a stiff and slightly shiny finish. It is used for evening dresses and wedding attire.

Brocade:

A richly decorative fabric, often made with silk, gold, or silver threads, known for its intricate raised designs, popular in luxury clothing and furnishings.

Each fabric has its strengths and limitations, and the choice depends on individual needs, occasion, and personal preferences. Understanding the properties of each type of fabric helps not only in selecting clothing items but also in ensuring their longevity and maximizing comfort and style.

CHOOSING THE RIGHT FABRIC FOR OCCASIONS AND BODY TYPES

Choosing the right fabric for different occasions and body types is a crucial aspect to ensure that clothing not only looks aesthetically pleasing but is also comfortable and suitable for its purpose. Each fabric has characteristics that can influence how a garment falls and fits on the body, as well as its appropriateness for specific events or contexts. Here is a detailed guide on how to select the most suitable fabric based on the occasion and body type:

Formal Occasions:

In formal occasions, fabric choice becomes a statement of style and attention to detail, reflecting the significance of the event. For such moments, like weddings, gala dinners, award nights, or high-level business meetings, fabrics must not only look impeccable but also feel luxurious to the touch and perfectly adapt to the context.

Silk, with its glossy surface and fluid drape, is often the preferred choice for evening gowns and cocktail dresses. Its innate sophistication and a variety of weaves available, from smooth satin to lightweight and airy chiffon, offer a wide range of options for different types of formal attire. Silk also has the advantage of being incredibly versatile in terms of colors and prints, allowing for the creation of attention-grabbing dresses that leave a lasting impression.

Linen, traditionally considered more casual, is gaining popularity in formal summer occasions due to its lightweight and breathability. Linen dresses and suits can offer an elegant and comfortable alternative for outdoor weddings, corporate events, or other formal functions in warm environments. The key lies in choosing high-quality linens that are less prone to wrinkling, maintaining a clean and sophisticated appearance.

Brocade and velvet, both rich and textured fabrics, are excellent choices for adding a sense of luxury and depth to a formal outfit. Brocade, with its intricate raised designs, is perfect for tuxedo jackets, evening dresses, and accessories. Velvet, on the other hand, is ideal for winter dresses, evening jackets, and formal pants, offering a sense of warmth and opulence.

Furthermore, for formal events, it is crucial to consider the fit and tailoring of clothing. A well-tailored suit in high-quality fabric not only looks elegant but also enhances the confidence of the wearer. The right fabric choice, coupled with impeccable tailoring, can make a difference at a formal event, ensuring a look that is both refined and representative of one's personal style.

Casual and Everyday Occasions:

In the realm of casual and everyday occasions, fabric selection plays a crucial role in ensuring that clothing is not only stylistically appropriate but also practical and comfortable for daily wear. In these situations, where comfort and ease of maintenance are a priority, chosen fabrics should be able to withstand daily wear while remaining fresh and pleasant to wear.

Cotton stands out as one of the most versatile and reliable choices for everyday clothing. It is a natural fabric that excels in breathability, making it ideal for a wide range of weather conditions. In summer, lightweight cotton is an excellent choice for shirts, dresses, and shorts, providing relief from heat and humidity. For colder months, heavier cotton like flannel offers warmth and comfort. Additionally, cotton's resistance and ease of care make it particularly suitable for daily use.

Denim, with its iconic reputation in casual fashion, is another key fabric for everyday wear. Appreciated for its durability and timeless style, denim is perfect for jeans, jackets, and even skirts.

It pairs well with a variety of outfits, from entirely casual looks to slightly more sophisticated ones, and evolves aesthetically with wear, gaining character and personality over time.

In addition to these, other fabrics like cotton jersey, viscose, and lyocell are popular choices for casual clothing. They are lightweight, soft on the skin, and offer great freedom of movement, making them ideal for t-shirts, casual dresses, and comfortable pants. These fabrics are also relatively easy to care for, making them practical for daily use.

Ultimately, when it comes to casual and everyday occasions, fabric choices should balance style and functionality. Fabrics like cotton and denim not only provide comfort and durability but also offer the opportunity to explore various styles and fashion trends in daily wear. Choosing the right fabrics for these occasions means ensuring that your clothing is practical, comfortable, and suitable for the active and varied lifestyle of everyday life.

Sports and Outdoor Activities:

In the context of sports and outdoor activities, fabric selection becomes essential to ensure performance, comfort, and durability. Sportswear must address a variety of challenges, from extreme weather conditions to the need to support a wide range of movements. Therefore, fabrics used in these contexts are often at the forefront in terms of technology and functionality.

Nylon and polyester are two of the most commonly used fabrics in sportswear. Both are synthetic fabrics known for their strength and durability. Nylon, in particular, is appreciated for its exceptional resistance to wear and tear, making it ideal for outdoor activities like hiking and cycling. It is also relatively lightweight and offers some water resistance, which is useful in variable weather conditions.

Polyester, on the other hand, is particularly known for its excellent moisture-wicking properties. It can draw sweat away from the skin, transferring it to the fabric's surface where it can evaporate quickly. This "breathable" effect helps to keep the body dry and comfortable during physical exercise, making it a frequent choice for running gear, gym wear, and other sportswear.

The addition of spandex or elastane to these fabrics is another important consideration in sportswear. This fiber is remarkably elastic and can stretch to many times its original length, then return to its initial shape. This elasticity ensures an excellent fit and unparalleled freedom of movement, which is essential in many sports activities.

Other innovative fabrics that are gaining popularity in sportswear include materials such as breathable mesh fabric, which offers superior ventilation, and technological fabrics that can provide UV protection or antibacterial properties.

For outdoor activities, in addition to resistance and moisture management, protection from the elements may also need to be considered. Fabrics with waterproof or wind-resistant properties are essential for garments intended for hiking, mountaineering, or other outdoor activities.

In summary, fabric choices for sportswear and outdoor activities require careful consideration of a range of factors, including strength, moisture management, elasticity, and protection from the elements. With continuous innovation in textile materials, sportswear and outdoor clothing are becoming increasingly sophisticated, offering athletes and outdoor enthusiasts the performance and comfort they need to excel in their activities.

Hot Climates:

In hot environments or during the summer months, wearing

suitable fabrics is essential to maintain comfort and prevent overheating. The choice of the right materials can make the difference between feeling suffocated and sweaty or cool and comfortable. Ideal fabrics for hot climates and summer are those that combine lightweight, breathability, and moisture-wicking capabilities, helping to regulate body temperature and keep the skin dry.

Linen:

Linen is one of the most classic fabrics for hot weather. It is extremely breathable and has excellent moisture-absorbing abilities, making it perfect for hot and humid days. Linen is also known for its durability and strength. Although it tends to wrinkle easily, this characteristic is often accepted as part of its natural and casual charm.

Lightweight Cotton:

Cotton, particularly in its lighter forms, is another ideal fabric for hot weather. Fabrics like cotton voile, batiste, or chambray are lightweight and allow for good air circulation, helping to keep the body cool. Additionally, cotton is soft on the skin, making it comfortable for extended wear, and it is also easy to wash and maintain.

Rayon/Viscose:

Rayon or viscose, made from cellulose, are popular choices for summer clothing due to their lightweight and fluid nature. These fabrics drape well and offer a feeling of freshness against the skin, although they are not as effective as linen or cotton in managing moisture.

Seersucker and Fabrics:

Seersucker is a cotton fabric that features a crinkled texture, which helps keep the material away from the skin, increasing air circulation and reducing stickiness. Other woven fabrics, like those with wide knits or mesh construction, can also be good choices for hot climates due to their ability to allow air to pass through.

Mixed Fabrics:

Some mixed fabrics that combine natural fibers with synthetic fibers can offer the benefits of breathability and lightweightness along with increased wrinkle resistance and easy maintenance.

When choosing clothing for hot climates, in addition to considering the type of fabric, it's also important to think about the color and cut of the garments. Light colors reflect sunlight rather than absorbing it, helping to keep the body cooler. Loose and flowing styles that allow for greater air circulation around the body are also practical choices to stay fresh.

In conclusion, wearing the right fabrics in hot climates is essential to stay comfortable, cool, and dry. By selecting materials like linen, lightweight cotton, and rayon, and opting for light colors and relaxed cuts, you can fully enjoy summer activities while maintaining an elegant and comfortable style.

Cold Climates:

During the colder months, it's essential to choose fabrics that not only provide warmth and comfort but also protect against harsh weather conditions. In cold climates, the fabrics you choose for clothing should be capable of retaining body heat, offering good insulation, and ideally managing moisture to keep the body dry.

Fabrics like wool and cashmere are among the top choices for their combination of warmth, style, and comfort.

Wool:

Wool is an extremely versatile and functional fabric for cold weather. It is naturally insulating and capable of retaining body heat, making it perfect for sweaters, coats, scarves, and gloves. Wool also has the ability to absorb moisture, keeping the body dry and comfortable. Varieties of wool include merino wool, alpaca wool, and mohair, each with its unique characteristics in terms of texture, weight, and warmth.

Merino Wool:

Merino wool is particularly appreciated for its fineness and softness, making it ideal for garments in direct contact with the skin, such as lightweight sweaters and thermal underwear. It's less itchy than other wools and has excellent temperature-regulating properties, making it suitable for both inner and outer layers.

Cashmere:

Cashmere is known for its extraordinary softness and luxury. It's lighter than traditional wool but offers superior insulation, making it an excellent choice for high-quality sweaters, scarves, and hats. Despite its higher price, cashmere is a valuable investment due to its durability and the comfort it provides.

Flannel and Tweed:

Flannel, a slightly fuzzy fabric made of wool or cotton, is another popular choice for cold weather. It's warm and soft, ideal for casual shirts and pajamas. Tweed, a thick and durable wool fabric, is suitable for outerwear and pants, providing both warmth and durability.

Synthetic and Mixed Fabrics:

Synthetic fabrics like polyester can be used in winter clothing, often as part of mixed fabrics, to increase resistance to water and wind. Many modern outerwear garments include a blend of synthetic and natural materials to maximize warmth, lightweightness, and protection from the elements.

Layering with Different Fabrics:

In dressing for cold weather, layering is an effective strategy. Combining different layers of fabrics can provide not only additional insulation but also versatility, allowing you to adapt to temperature variations throughout the day.

In conclusion, choosing the right fabrics for cold climates is crucial to stay warm, dry, and comfortable. Investing in quality fabrics like wool, cashmere, and technical blends can significantly enhance the winter dressing experience, enabling you to face the cold with style and comfort.

Body Types and Fit:

Choosing the fabric in relation to body type and fit is a fundamental aspect of creating an outfit that not only fits well but also enhances the wearer's figure. Each body type has its unique characteristics, and understanding how different fabrics can accentuate or minimize certain areas can make a significant difference in the overall appearance of clothing.

Curvy Figures:

For those with a curvier figure, fabrics that naturally drape and flow along the body can be particularly flattering. Fabrics like chiffon, lightweight silk, or jersey have a soft drape that follows the body's lines without clinging too tightly. These materials can gently wrap around curves, subtly emphasizing them. Avoid fabrics that are too stiff or heavy, as they may add unwanted volume or not fit well around curves.

Petite or Slim Figures:

For those with a slimmer or petite figure, fabrics with more structure or texture can be advantageous. Fabrics like tweed, thick cotton, or even fabrics with a certain rigidity, like some types of denim, can add volume and definition where needed. These fabrics can help create the illusion of more pronounced curves or structure in the physique.

Tall and Slim Figures:

For tall and slim figures, experimenting with a variety of fabrics can be an excellent choice. Lightweight and flowing fabrics can add movement and softness, while heavier fabrics or those with some texture can add visual interest and substance to the outfit.

Generous Figures:

For those with a figure with more generous proportions, choosing fabrics that offer good structure without being too rigid is ideal. Fabrics that offer some degree of stretch, like a cotton and elastane blend, can provide comfort and a fit that enhances the figure.

Considering Fit and Comfort:

Regardless of body type, it's crucial that the chosen fabric is comfortable and fits well. A fabric that doesn't fit correctly can compromise both the appearance and comfort of the outfit.

Adaptability for Different Occasions:

It's also important to consider how a fabric can adapt to different occasions. For example, a more formal fabric might be more suitable for the office or formal events, while a more casual and relaxed fabric might be ideal for leisure time.

In conclusion, choosing the right fabric in relation to body type and fit requires careful consideration of one's proportions and personal preferences. Experimenting with different fabrics and understanding how each can enhance different figures is essential for creating a wardrobe that not only looks fantastic but also makes you feel comfortable and confident in every situation.

Comfort and Personal Preferences:

In addition to considering the aesthetic aspect, it's essential to choose fabrics that make you feel comfortable. Skin sensitivity, personal preferences, and overall comfort are all important aspects to consider when selecting fabric.

In conclusion, choosing the right fabric based on the occasion and body type is a combination of functionality, aesthetics, and personal comfort. Understanding the properties and qualities of different fabrics will allow you to make more informed choices and create outfits that not only look fantastic but also perfectly suit your needs and lifestyle.

FREQUENTLY ASKED QUESTIONS: WHAT FABRICS ARE BEST FOR DIFFERENT SEASONS?

Choosing the right fabric based on the season is a fundamental aspect to ensure comfort, practicality, and adaptability to weather conditions. Each season has its own characteristics that influence which fabric is most suitable. Here is a guide on which fabrics are generally considered the best for different seasons:

Spring:

Spring is characterized by variable temperatures and unpredictable weather. Lightweight fabrics that offer some protection are ideal.

- **Cotton**: Breathable and comfortable, it is suitable for the variability of spring.

- **Linen**: Provides freshness on warmer days but can be layered for cooler weather.

- **Lightweight Wool Blends:** For cooler days, lightweight wool blends offer warmth without overheating.

Summer:

During the summer, lightweight and breathable fabrics are essential to stay cool.

- **Linen and Lightweight Cotton**: Great for their moisture-absorbing properties and keeping the skin cool.

- **Rayon/Viscose**: Good for its lightweight feel and ability to wick away sweat.

- **Seersucker**: Its crinkled texture keeps the fabric away from the skin, increasing air circulation.

Fall:

Fall requires fabrics that can adapt to cooler weather and temperature variations.

- **Tweed and Flannel**: Provide warmth and are perfect for autumn weather.

- **Denim and Heavy Cotton**: Offer a good balance between warmth and breathability.

- **Lightweight Knits**: Sweaters and cardigans can be easily layered to adjust to variable temperatures.

Winter:

In winter, it's essential to choose fabrics that retain heat.

- **Wool and Cashmere**: Offer excellent thermal insulation.

- **Velvet and Heavy Tweed**: Ideal for outerwear due to their density and wind-blocking capabilities.

- **Insulating Technical Fabrics**: Many modern winter outerwear uses advanced synthetic fabrics that provide warmth without the weight of traditional fabrics.

Remember that fabric choice should also consider personal comfort and individual sensitivity. Some people may find certain fabrics more comfortable or better suited to their personal style than others. Additionally, layering different fabrics can help navigate temperature fluctuations within the same season.

DEBUNKING MYTHS: THE MOST EXPENSIVE FABRICS ARE ALWAYS THE BEST

Debunking the myth that the most expensive fabrics are always the best is a widespread misconception but doesn't always align with reality. While it's true that quality often comes at a price, price alone is not the sole indicator of a fabric's superiority. Here are some key points to debunk this myth:

Quality vs. Branding:

Many expensive fabrics carry high price tags due to branding or designer associations rather than the intrinsic quality of the material. A fabric produced by a luxury brand may have a higher price compared to a similar one offered by a less-known brand, even though the quality is comparable.

Production Cost vs. Performance:

Some fabrics are expensive due to their complex production process or the rarity of raw materials. However, this doesn't automatically imply that they are more performance-oriented or suitable for all occasions compared to less expensive fabrics. For example, cashmere is known for its softness and warmth, but for some activities or weather conditions, merino wool or even an advanced synthetic might be a better choice.

Durability and Maintenance:

Some expensive fabrics, like fine silks or fabrics with delicate embroidery, may require more careful care and might not be as durable as less expensive, sturdier fabrics. For everyday use or garments that require simple maintenance, less expensive fabrics can be more practical and cost-effective.

Personal Comfort and Preferences:

Personal comfort and preferences play a crucial role in fabric selection. A less expensive fabric that fits well and feels comfortable against the skin may be a better choice than a more expensive option that doesn't meet the same personal needs.

Sustainability and Ethics:

In some cases, less expensive fabrics may be produced in a more sustainable or ethical manner compared to luxury fabrics. The growing focus on eco-friendly fabrics and ethical production is changing how we assess the quality and value of fabrics.

In conclusion, while expensive fabrics may offer certain benefits like exclusivity, refined finishes, or a particular prestige associated with the brand, they are not automatically the best choice for every situation or individual. Fabric selection should be based on a variety of factors, including quality, functionality, comfort, durability, and personal preferences, rather than just price alone.

HUMAN FIGURE CHARACTERISTICS

In the world of fashion and personal style, a thorough understanding of human figure characteristics is essential for creating outfits that are not only aesthetically pleasing but also enhance each individual's uniqueness. Every person has a distinct body type with their own proportions and features that can be highlighted or harmonized through conscious clothing choices.

The human figure can be classified into different types, each with its specificities. These categories are useful as guidelines to better understand how different clothing styles can adapt to or enhance various body shapes. Here is a general overview of some of the most common types:

Hourglass Figure:

Characterized by shoulders and hips of approximately the same width and a defined waist. This body type is considered proportionally balanced.

Pear or Triangle Figure:

Distinguished by wider hips compared to shoulders and chest. The lower part of the body is more prominent than the upper part.

Inverted Triangle Figure:

This body type has broader shoulders compared to the hips. The upper body is more dominant, while the lower part is relatively narrower.

Rectangle Figure:

Characterized by shoulders, waist, and hips of approximately the same width, giving a straighter and less curvy impression.

Apple or Oval Figure:

Identified by a wider central body section compared to shoulders and hips. The waist area is less defined.

Understanding your body type is the first step in choosing clothes that not only fit well but also enhance your natural features. It's important to note that these categories are simplifications, and every individual has unique characteristics that may not fit perfectly into a single category. Furthermore, fashion is not just about conforming to certain rules; it's also a personal expression and a way to explore and play with different shapes and styles.

In the following sections, we will delve into specific guides on how to dress different body types, providing advice on how to highlight your unique features and use clothing to create visual balance. Additionally, we will debunk some common myths about body types and clothing, emphasizing that fashion is for everyone, and every person can freely express themselves through style.

GUIDE ON HOW TO DRESS DIFFERENT BODY TYPES

The guide on how to dress different body types is a crucial element for anyone involved in fashion, especially personal shoppers. This knowledge allows you to choose clothes that not only fit perfectly but also enhance the individual characteristics of each client. Here's a detailed guide on dressing different body types:

Hourglass Body Type:

The hourglass body type is considered one of the most proportionate and harmonious, with a well-defined waist and shoulders and hips of approximately the same width. Here are some detailed tips to make the most of this figure:

Dresses and Tops:

  - **Fitted or empire-cut dresses**: These styles emphasize the slim waist and flow gracefully over the hips, highlighting natural curves.

  - **Blouses and tops with belts or waistbands**: These elements further accentuate the waist, creating a focal point that enhances natural proportions.

  - **Necklines**: Choose necklines that enhance the bust, such as V-necks, sweetheart necklines, or wrap styles, which can add a feminine and sophisticated touch to the outfit.

Pants and Skirts:

  - **High-waisted jeans and trousers**: These help define the waist and emphasize the hourglass shape, especially when paired with tucked-in tops.

  - **Pencil skirts**: They follow the body's curves, emphasizing feminine lines and creating an elegant and professional look.

- **A-line or flared skirts**: They can balance the figure and add a playful touch while maintaining waist definition.

Jackets and Blazers:

- **Tailored blazers and jackets**: Those that follow the waistline are ideal for maintaining balanced proportions and enhancing the figure.

- **Jackets with belts or slightly tapered at the waist**: These styles can further emphasize the hourglass shape.

Fabrics and Textures:

- **Fabrics that drape naturally and flow well**: Such as silk, rayon, and lightweight jersey, can accentuate curves without adding excessive volume.

Accessories:

- **Belts and sashes**: These are excellent for further emphasizing the waist. Choose medium-sized belts to create visual balance.

- **Necklaces and scarves**: They can be used to direct attention towards the face and bust, balancing the outfit.

Avoid:

- **Overly loose dresses and tops**: These can hide the definition of the waist and alter the balance of natural proportions.

- **Fabrics that are too rigid or bulky**: They can add unwanted bulk to certain areas, masking the natural silhouette.

Remember that while these tips are designed to enhance the hourglass body type, fashion is also an expression of individual personality. Therefore, it's important to choose clothes that not only enhance the figure but also reflect your personal style and make you feel comfortable and confident.

Pear Body Type:

For the pear-shaped body type, characterized by wider hips compared to shoulders and the bust, the goal in clothing is to visually balance the figure by highlighting the upper body and harmonizing the lower part. Here are some detailed tips:

Tops and Blouses:

- **Colors and Prints**: Choose tops in bright colors, bold prints, or decorative details like ruffles, elaborate collars, or sequins. These elements draw attention to the upper body.

- **Necklines**: Opt for necklines that visually widen the shoulders, such as boat necks, V-necks, or off-shoulder styles.

- **Tops with Volume or Structure**: Blouses or sweaters with details like puff sleeves, ruffles, or layers can add volume to the bust, balancing the hips.

Jackets and Blazers:

- **Structure**: Well-structured blazers and jackets, especially those with light shoulder padding or shoulder details, can help create the illusion of broader shoulders, thus balancing the wider hips.

- **Length**: Jackets that end just above or at the mid-hips are ideal, as they help define the waist without adding volume to the hips.

Pants and Skirts:

   - **Straight Cuts and A-Line**: Choose skirts that fall straight from the hips or flared skirts to minimize hip width. Avoid skirts that are too tight or have excessive volume at the bottom.

   - **Straight-Leg or Bootcut Pants**: These styles can help balance hip width. Avoid overly tight pants or those with conspicuous details on the hips.

Accessories:

   - **Voluminous Necklaces and Scarves**: Bold accessories around the neck can draw attention upward.

   - **Shoulder Bags or Clutches**: Carry bags that sit on the upper body rather than at hip level.

Fabrics and Texture:

   - **Upper Body**: Fabrics with structure or visual details can add interest. Avoid fabrics that are too tight or thin.

   - **Lower Body**: Opt for flowing and draping fabrics that do not add extra volume to the hips.

Avoid:

   - **Bulky details on the hips**: Applied pockets, ruffles, horizontal hems, or large prints on the hips can further emphasize their width.

   - **Too short or tight skirts**: These can exaggerate the disparity between the upper and lower body.

Always remember that these are general guidelines, and it's

essential to choose garments that not only flatter the figure but also reflect your personal taste and comfort. Fashion should be a means of self-expression, so finding a balance between style recommendations and individual style is crucial.

Inverted Triangle Body Type:

For the inverted triangle body type, characterized by broad shoulders and relatively narrow hips, the goal in clothing is to create visual balance between the upper and lower body. This can be achieved by accentuating the hips and legs while minimizing shoulder width. Here are some specific tips to make the most of this body type:

Tops and Shirts:

- **Colors and Style**: Opt for tops in neutral or dark colors, which tend to minimize shoulder width. Choose styles with simple cuts and clean lines that do not add extra volume in the shoulder area.

- **Necklines**: V-neck or U-neck necklines can help visually reduce shoulder width, giving a more balanced appearance.

- **Avoid**: Puff sleeves, ruffles, or any detail that can add volume to the upper body.

Pants and Skirts:

- **Details and Colors**: Select pants or skirts with details, light colors, or prints to draw attention downward. This helps balance the figure.

- **Flared Skirts**: These skirts add volume to the hips, creating balance with broad shoulders.

- **Palazzo or Wide-Leg Pants**: They provide a contrast to broad shoulders and add volume to the lower body.

Jackets and Blazers:

- **Cut**: Choose jackets that are fitted at the waist and slightly flare out towards the bottom to balance proportions.

- **Avoid**: Jackets with padded shoulders or excessive structure that can further emphasize shoulder width.

Accessories:

- **Belts**: Use belts to emphasize the waist and add curves to the figure.

- **Shoulder or Clutch Bags:** Avoid bags that hang on the shoulder and opt for clutches or crossbody bags that fall at hip level.

Fabrics and Texture:

- **Lower Body**: Fabrics with structure or volume, such as pleated or chunky knit fabrics, can be useful in adding volume to the hips.

- **Upper Body**: Choose soft and draping fabrics that do not add extra volume to the shoulders.

Shoes:

- **Style**: Shoes with bold details or colors can draw attention downward, helping to balance the figure.

As with any body type, the key is to experiment with different styles and find what not only flatters the figure but also reflects personal taste. Fashion should be a means of self-expression, so dressing in a way that makes you feel comfortable and confident is essential.

Rectangular Body Type:

For the rectangular body type, characterized by shoulders, waist, and hips of approximately the same width, the goal in clothing is to create the illusion of curves and define the waist to break the linearity of the silhouette. Here are some detailed tips to make the most of this body type:

Waist Definition:

- **Belts and Sashes**: Use belts or sashes to cinch the waist on dresses and tops. This helps create definition and gives the illusion of a curvier figure.

- **Dresses with Waist Details:** Dresses with details like pleats, drapes, built-in belts, or cuts that emphasize the waist can help create a more curvaceous look.

Creating Volume:

- **Tops and Blouses**: Choose tops with details such as ruffles, gathers, or voluminous sleeves to add volume to the upper body.

- **Skirts and Pants**: Opt for flared skirts, pleated skirts, or wide-leg pants to add volume and movement to the lower body.

Layering and Texture:

- **Layering**: Use layering of different garments to add visual interest and depth. For example, a cardigan or a lightweight jacket over a shirt can create a more dynamic silhouette.

- **Diverse Textures**: Experiment with fabrics of different textures and weights. Fabrics like tweed, velvet, or knits can add an interesting visual element.

Peplum Dresses:

- **Peplum**: Dresses or blouses with peplum add volume around the hips, creating the illusion of more curves.

Accessories:

- **Scarves and Necklaces:** Use accessories like long scarves or statement necklaces to add a focal point and break the linearity of the body.

Dress Lines and Cuts:

- **Fitted Dresses**: Choose dresses with a fitted cut or seams that simulate curves to create the illusion of a more shapely figure.

Avoid:

- **Tight-fitting dresses and tops**: These can emphasize the lack of natural curves. It's better to opt for garments that create volume and visual interest.

These tips are intended to help enhance and celebrate the rectangular body type. However, it's important to remember that fashion rules are flexible, and personal expression and comfort should always be a priority. Experimenting with different styles and finding what works best for your personality and comfort is essential to create a look that is both flattering and true to yourself.

Apple or Oval Body Type:

For the apple or oval body type, characterized by a wider central area compared to shoulders and hips, the main goal in clothing is to minimize width around the waist area and highlight other parts of the body, such as the shoulders and legs. Here are some tips on how to dress this body type effectively:

Tops and Blouses:

 - **Necklines**: V-neck or U-neck necklines are ideal because they help elongate the neck and reduce the width of the bust. This type of neckline can also draw attention to the face.

 - **Length**: Tops that end just below the hip line can help create a more elongated silhouette.

 - **Loose Fits**: Tops that fall freely over the central part of the body, without clinging too much, can mask width and create a more fluid line.

Pants and Skirts:

 - **Straight-Leg or Slightly Tapered Pants**: These styles can help balance the figure, especially when chosen in dark colors or fluid fabrics.

 - **A-Line Skirts**: Skirts that gently widen from the hips can balance the upper body.

 - **Avoid**: Pants or skirts with bulky details around the waist area, such as large pockets or decorative belts, which can add unwanted volume.

Dresses:

 - **Empire or High-Waisted Dresses**: These dresses can help lift attention away from the central area and create a more elongated line.

 - **Draped Dresses**: Fabrics that drape can be flattering, especially if the draping starts from the upper body.

Jackets and Blazers:

- **Open and Loose Cuts**: Jackets and blazers that are not too structured can add structure without adding volume to the central part of the body.

- **Length**: Jackets that end around the hips or just above can be more flattering than those that are too short or too long.

Accessories:

- **Long Necklaces and Scarves**: They can help create vertical lines that elongate the body.

- **Shoulder Bags**: Positioning the bag to hang sideways can help balance the figure.

Fabrics and Texture:

- **Soft and Flowing Fabrics**: These are preferable to rigid fabrics as they drape better on the body and minimize emphasis on width.

Avoid:

- **Fabrics that are too tight or clingy**: These can highlight the central part of the body.

- **Large and bulky prints:** On the central part of the body, they can visually add volume.

These tips are intended to help those with an apple or oval body type feel comfortable and confident in their style, emphasizing their best features. However, it is essential to remember that clothing should reflect personal style and comfort, in addition to following any styling advice.

General Tips:

Fabrics: Choose fabrics that work in favor of your body type. Fluid and draping fabrics can be flattering for some, while others may benefit from more structured fabrics.

Colors and Prints: Use colors and prints to draw attention to your best features. Dark colors tend to slim, while light colors and vibrant prints can emphasize. In any case, the most important thing is that the individual feels comfortable and confident in their clothes. These guidelines are intended as a starting point for exploring and experimenting with fashion. It's crucial to remember that fashion rules are flexible, and personal expression and comfort should always be prioritized.

TIPS ON ENHANCEMENT AND CAMOUFLAGE

Enhancing and camouflaging certain body features through clothing is a fundamental technique for anyone looking to express their personal style to the fullest while feeling comfortable and confident. Here are some tips on how to highlight strengths and minimize areas you wish to downplay:

Enhancement:

- **Strengths**: Identify your strengths. This could be your neck, shoulders, waist, legs, or any other area you like the most. Wear clothes that draw attention to these areas.

- **Colors and Prints**: Use bright colors and interesting prints to draw attention to your best features. For example, if you want to enhance your bust, you might wear a shirt with an eye-catching print.

- **Cuts and Silhouette**: Choose cuts that accentuate your features. For example, if you have a slim waist, emphasize it with belts or dresses that cinch at this point.

Camouflage:

- **Minimize Specific Areas**: If there are areas of your body you prefer to minimize, use dark colors, simple cuts, and non-clinging fabrics for those areas.

- **Balance and Proportion**: Create balance and proportions with your clothing. If you have broad shoulders, for example, balance the silhouette with A-line skirts or wide-legged pants.

- **Layering and Texture**: Use layering and different textures to camouflage areas like the abdomen or hips. A long cardigan or an open jacket can be very helpful in this regard.

Use of Accessories:

- **Distraction with Accessories:** Use accessories to divert attention from areas you prefer not to emphasize. For example, statement necklaces or scarves can draw attention to your face and away from the central part of the body.

- **Bags and Shoes**: Bags and shoes can be used to balance the figure. For example, if you want to add volume to the lower body, try wearing shoes with bold details.

Choice of Fabrics:

- **Flowing Fabrics for Camouflage**: Soft and flowing fabrics can drape elegantly, concealing areas you don't want to highlight.

- **Structured Fabrics for Enhancement**: Fabrics with some structure can help enhance the areas of the body you want to emphasize.

Fitting and Adjustments:

- **Perfect Fitting**: Make sure your clothes have the perfect fit. Well-fitting attire can make a significant difference in how you enhance or camouflage certain areas of the body.

Remember, these are general tips, and every person is unique. It's important to experiment with different styles and garments to find what works best for you, always keeping in mind that clothing should reflect your personality and make you feel comfortable and confident.

FREQUENTLY ASKED QUESTIONS: HOW CAN I CHOOSE CLOTHES THAT SUIT MY BODY TYPE?

Choosing clothes that suit your body type is a common and important question. Here are some key steps and considerations to keep in mind to help you make fashion choices that enhance your figure:

Know Your Body Type:

- First and foremost, it's important to identify your body type. Observe the proportions between your shoulders, waist, and hips. Common body types include hourglass, pear, inverted triangle, rectangle, and apple.

Accentuate Your Strengths:

- Identify areas of your body that you want to emphasize. You may have well-defined shoulders, a slim waist, long legs, etc. Choose clothing that highlights these strengths.

Balance Proportions:

- If your goal is to create visual balance, choose clothing that helps balance the proportions of your body. For example, if you have a pear-shaped figure, you can balance wider hips with bright or embellished tops.

Choose Appropriate Fabrics and Colors:

- Fabrics can have a significant impact on how a garment fits and drapes on the body. Select fabrics that flatter your figure without adding unwanted volume. Colors also play an important role; dark colors tend to slim, while light colors and prints can draw attention to specific areas.

Try Different Styles and Cuts:

- There is no one-size-fits-all rule. It's important to experiment with different styles and cuts to see what works best for you. Try different silhouettes, from fitted to more flowing, to discover what makes you feel most comfortable and confident.

Fitting and Adjustments:

- Good fitting is crucial. Regardless of your body type, clothes should fit well and feel comfortable. Don't hesitate to make minor tailoring adjustments for a perfect fit.

Personal Style and Comfort:

- Finally, your personal style and comfort are the most important factors. Choose clothing that reflects your personality and makes you feel secure and comfortable.

Remember, the key is to wear what makes you feel good. Fashion is a means to express yourself, so choose clothes that speak to your unique personality.

DEBUNKING MYTHS: ONLY CERTAIN BODY TYPES CAN WEAR SPECIFIC STYLES

Debunking the myth that only certain body types can wear specific styles is an outdated and limiting concept in modern fashion. This idea implies that there are strict rules about what people can or cannot wear based on their body shape, which is not only restrictive but also ignores individual diversity and uniqueness. Here are some points to debunk this myth:

Personal Style Beyond "Rules":

- Fashion is self-expression and should be fun and liberating, not limiting. Everyone should feel free to explore different styles regardless of their body shape.

Adaptation Rather Than Limitation:

- Instead of restricting oneself to certain styles, it is possible to adapt various styles to better suit one's body. This can include tailoring modifications or simply choosing different cuts of the same type of clothing.

Confidence Is Key:

- Often, what matters most is not the body type but how one carries a garment. Confidence in wearing a particular style can have a greater impact on the overall appearance than body shape.

Fashion Evolution:

- Fashion is constantly evolving and becoming more inclusive. There have been many initiatives and movements in the fashion world that encourage people to wear what they love, regardless of their size or body shape.

Experimentation and Exploration:

It is essential to experiment with different styles and find what works best for you. Fashion is a way to express individuality and should be accessible to everyone, regardless of body type.

HOW TO CONDUCT A CONSULTATION PART 1 AND PART 2

Conducting an image consultation requires a well-structured and personalized approach that takes into account the client's needs, desires, and lifestyle. Here's how to proceed:

Part 1: Preparation and Initial Assessment

Initial Meeting:

- The first step is an introductory meeting with the client. This can take place in person or virtually. The goal is to understand the client's needs, goals, and expectations.

Analysis of Current Style:

- Evaluate the client's current style. This may include an analysis of the existing wardrobe, style preferences, and shopping habits.

Discussion of Goals:

- Discuss the client's goals, whether it's a wardrobe update, preparation for a specific event, or the need for an image change due to a new phase in life.

Body Type and Color Assessment:

- Analyze the client's body type and the color palette that suits them best. This will help in selecting clothing that enhances their figure.

Budget and Preferences:

- Discuss the budget and shopping preferences. It's important to establish a realistic budget that aligns with the client's needs.

Part 2: Planning and Implementation

Creating an Action Plan:

- Based on the gathered information, create an action plan. This may involve wardrobe cleaning, purchasing new clothing, or restyling existing garments.

Shopping and Garment Selection:

- Based on the budget and the client's style, select garments that align with their goals. This may include personal shopping or assisting with online shopping.

Fittings and Adjustments:

- Organize fitting sessions to ensure the new garments fit perfectly. Some tailoring adjustments may be necessary.

Mixing and Matching:

- Assist the client in combining new and existing garments to create complete outfits. Provide advice on mixing and matching to maximize the wardrobe.

Follow-up:

- After implementing the plan, schedule a follow-up with the client to assess the results and make any necessary changes or adjustments.

The goal of an image consultation is to leave the client with a renewed sense of confidence and a wardrobe that truly reflects their personality and lifestyle.

CONSULTATION PROCESS FROM BEGINNING TO END

The image consulting process is a structured journey aimed at transforming and enhancing the client's personal image. This process may vary slightly depending on each client's specific needs, but generally follows a logical sequence from start to finish:

Initial Phase: Consultation and Assessment

The initial phase of an image consultation is crucial to establish a solid foundation for the future success of the process. This phase consists of two main parts: the initial consultation and the analysis of the current wardrobe.

During the initial consultation, a personalized approach is essential. Each client has unique image goals and style preferences. Understanding these aspects is crucial for effective consulting. The consultant should ask targeted questions to gain a clear understanding of the client's expectations, daily habits, typical environments, and which aspects of their style they wish to improve or change. It is also important to discuss personal preferences regarding colors, fabrics, and preferred cuts, as these details provide valuable insights into what the client feels comfortable in and which new directions can be explored.

Analyzing the current wardrobe involves a detailed review of the client's existing wardrobe. Specific pieces are assessed for their fit, style, and how often they are worn. Part of the analysis is identifying strengths in the current wardrobe, such as garments the client loves and feels good wearing, which can serve as a foundation for new purchases. It is also crucial to recognize what is missing in the wardrobe or what is no longer in line with the client's image goals, such as outdated items, items that no longer fit, or no longer reflect the client's current style or life stage. In some cases, wardrobe decluttering may be necessary by removing items that are no longer worn or do not fit the style objectives.

This initial phase is fundamental for an effective and satisfying transformation of the client's wardrobe and style, requiring careful listening, observation, and the ability to create a customized strategy that aligns with the client's vision and individual needs.

Planning and Plan Development

In the planning and plan development phase of an image consultation, the consultant and client work together to define specific goals and create an action plan that reflects the client's needs and aspirations. This step is crucial to ensure that the final result aligns with what the client desires and requires.

Goal Definition:

Goal definition is a collaborative process. The consultant guides the client in reflecting on what they want to achieve from the consultation. This can vary greatly depending on the client: some may seek a complete wardrobe overhaul, while others may focus on optimizing their clothing for specific occasions, such as corporate events, ceremonies, or daily life.

It is important that these goals are clear, measurable, and realistic. The consultant can help the client set priorities and distinguish between short-term and long-term goals.

Personalized Action Plan:

Once the goals are defined, the next step is the development of a personalized action plan. This plan is a living document and can be adapted during the consultation based on client feedback and changes in goals.

The plan may include various elements, such as cleaning and

organizing the existing wardrobe, which helps make space for new items and rediscover forgotten pieces that can be reused or adapted.

The purchase of new clothing is another crucial aspect of the plan. The consultant suggests pieces that fit the client's style objectives, considering factors like budget, personal preferences, body type, and usage occasions.

Combining outfits is an essential element, as it helps the client visualize how different pieces can be paired to create various looks. This includes mixing and matching existing garments with new purchases to maximize wardrobe versatility.

Advice on colors and styles is provided to guide the client towards choices that enhance their image. This can include selecting colors that complement the client's skin tone, as well as suggestions on styles and cuts that suit their body type and lifestyle.

In conclusion, the planning and plan development phase is a dynamic and interactive process that lays the groundwork for an effective and personalized transformation of the client's wardrobe and style.

Implementation

The implementation phase in an image consultation is where the previously established plans and strategies come to life through concrete actions. This stage is essential for achieving the desired change in the client's image and wardrobe.

Shopping:

Shopping is a critical moment where the clothing that will constitute the client's new wardrobe is selected. This activity can be carried out in different ways. Some consultants prefer to personally accompany clients to physical stores, offering immediate style, fit, and combination advice. Alternatively, especially if the client has time constraints or preferences for online shopping, the consultant can provide suggestions and links for online purchases, often selecting items directly from websites and retailers.

During shopping, it is important to keep an eye on the budget and ensure that each purchase aligns with the set style goals. The consultant must balance between the client's immediate desires and the long-term needs of their wardrobe.

Adjustments and Alterations:

A fundamental aspect is ensuring that each new garment fits perfectly. This may require tailoring adjustments, especially for key pieces like jackets, pants, or formal dresses. The consultant can collaborate with professional tailors to make the necessary alterations, ensuring that each garment fits beautifully on the client's body.

This attention to detail not only enhances the appearance of the garments but also contributes to the client's comfort and confidence.

Building the Wardrobe:

The ultimate goal is to help the client build a functional, versatile wardrobe that aligns with their lifestyle and image goals. This includes selecting garments that can be easily combined into different outfits, reducing the daily stress of choosing what to wear.

The consultant can also provide advice on how to maintain and care for new clothing, ensuring that they remain in good condition over time.

In conclusion, the implementation phase is a mix of strategic shopping, customization through adjustments, and the careful creation of a wardrobe that reflects and enhances the client's personal image. This phase requires careful planning, attention to detail, and a good dose of creativity.

Follow-Up and Evaluation

The follow-up and evaluation phase is an essential element in image consulting, as it allows for the verification of the effectiveness of the work done and ensures complete client satisfaction. This phase is as important as the previous ones, as it allows for refinement and perfection of the path taken.

Results Assessment:

After implementing the action plan and introducing wardrobe changes, the next step is to assess whether the set goals have been achieved. This includes an analysis of how the new garments fit into the client's lifestyle, whether they reflect their personal image, and whether they have contributed to improving their self-esteem and confidence.

Effective assessment can include comparing before-and-after photos, discussing reactions received from friends and colleagues, and self-evaluation by the client regarding how they feel with their new style.

Follow-Up:

Follow-up meetings are crucial for maintaining open and constructive communication with the client. These meetings can be used to discuss any challenges the client has encountered in adopting their new style or to address doubts about how to combine garments in different ways.

During these meetings, the consultant can offer additional advice and suggestions, and, if necessary, make adjustments to the action plan. For example, new needs or preferences that were not initially considered may arise.

This phase is also the opportunity to plan any future steps, such as seasonal wardrobe updates, additional shopping sessions, or outfit planning for specific events.

Follow-up and evaluation not only ensure that the results meet expectations but also strengthen the trust and collaboration relationship between the consultant and the client. This holistic approach guarantees that image consulting has a lasting and positive impact on the client, providing not only a service but also a transformative and enriching experience.

Ongoing Support:

Continued Advice: Providing ongoing support and advice to the client, helping them maintain and update their wardrobe over time.

The ultimate goal of an image consultation is to provide the client with the tools and confidence to express their personality through their style, ensuring that they feel comfortable and confident in their appearance on every occasion.

CUSTOMER COMMUNICATION TECHNIQUES

Customer communication techniques in an image consultancy are essential for building a relationship of trust and understanding, key elements for the success of the consultancy process. Effective communication goes beyond just conveying information; it also involves listening, interpreting, and responding to the needs and desires of the customer. Here are some key techniques:

Active Listening:

- The ability to actively listen is crucial. This means not only hearing what the customer is saying but also understanding the feelings and intentions behind the words. During consultations, it's important to give the customer plenty of time to express their concerns, desires, and expectations.

- Asking open-ended questions that encourage the customer to share more details about their lifestyle, personal preferences, and past experiences with fashion.

Empathy and Sensitivity:

- Showing empathy and sensitivity helps create a comfortable and open environment. Many customers can feel vulnerable when discussing their appearance and style, so it's important to show understanding and refrain from judgment.

- Customize the approach based on the customer's personality and needs. Every person is unique, and recognizing and respecting their individuality is crucial.

Clarity and Honesty:

- Communicating clearly and honestly helps set realistic

expectations. This includes being transparent about what can be achieved through image consultancy and the limitations of what can be done.

- Provide constructive and practical feedback. If a certain style or garment doesn't work for the customer, it's important to be honest but always in a kind and constructive manner.

Feedback and Adaptation:

- Encourage feedback from the customer and demonstrate openness to making changes based on their responses. Image consultancy is a dynamic and collaborative process.

- Be flexible and ready to adjust the action plan if it's discovered that the customer's preferences change during the consultancy.

Non-Verbal Communication:

- Pay attention to non-verbal communication as well. Body language, facial expressions, and tone of voice can provide important clues about how the customer feels about discussions and decisions made.

Ongoing Follow-Up:

- Maintain constant and regular communication through follow-ups via email, phone calls, or in-person meetings. This not only helps keep track of progress but also shows the customer that their journey is important and carefully followed.

Through effective communication, an image consultant can build a trusting relationship with the customer, deeply understand their needs, and work with them to achieve desired goals, ensuring a positive and transformative experience.

FREQUENTLY ASKED QUESTIONS: WHAT TO EXPECT DURING AN IMAGE CONSULTATION?

During an image consultation, clients can expect a detailed and personalized process aimed at improving and renewing their personal image. Here are some key aspects of what to expect:

Initial Meeting and Assessment: The initial meeting and assessment represent the cornerstone of the image consultation. During this fundamental meeting, the image consultant and the client establish the foundation for a collaborative and trusting relationship.

In this first meeting, the consultant adopts an active listening approach to deeply understand not only the client's style preferences but also their lifestyle, profession, daily activities, and social contexts. This insight helps create a clear picture of the client's needs and potential areas for improvement.

It's also the time for the client to share any insecurities or specific issues regarding their appearance or wardrobe. The client can discuss past experiences with fashion, what makes them comfortable, their clothing preferences and why, as well as any aspects they wish to change or improve.

The consultant can use this moment to set the goals of the consultation, working together with the client to determine what they want to achieve. This can range from a simple wardrobe update to a complete style change, focusing on professional attire or assistance for special occasions.

Additionally, the consultant can start outlining a preliminary strategy on how to proceed, which may include analyzing the existing wardrobe, planning for shopping, defining a personal style, and selecting colors and fabrics that best suit the client.

This meeting is also an opportunity to establish open and honest communication. It's important for the client to feel comfortable sharing thoughts and opinions, and for the consultant to create an environment where the client feels heard and valued.

In conclusion, the initial meeting and assessment are not only a moment of information exchange but also an opportunity to build a foundation of trust and understanding, crucial elements for a successful image consultation.

Wardrobe Analysis: Wardrobe analysis is a crucial step in image consultation, as it provides a concrete overview of the client's current style and areas that need improvement. This phase involves not only the physical analysis of garments in the wardrobe but also understanding how these pieces integrate into the client's lifestyle and needs.

During the analysis, the consultant examines each item in the client's wardrobe. This process involves evaluating fit, condition, color, and style of each piece. The consultant considers which pieces fit well and which are particularly flattering for the client's body type and skin tone.

A fundamental aspect of this phase is identifying garments that are no longer worn or that no longer reflect the client's current style or needs. These may include outdated items, those no longer suitable, or those that no longer spark joy or confidence in the client. The decision to keep, modify, or remove these items is made in collaboration with the client, always considering their feelings and emotions.

Furthermore, wardrobe analysis also serves to identify missing items. This can include basic pieces that form the foundation of a versatile wardrobe, such as quality shirts or well-tailored pants, or more specific items that could enhance the client's personal style.

The image consultant can also use this moment to teach the client how to combine different pieces to create new outfits, demonstrating how to maximize the use of each item. This includes explaining which color and fabric combinations work well together and how to build outfits that suit various occasions and seasons.

In conclusion, wardrobe analysis is a detailed process aimed at optimizing the client's existing wardrobe, eliminating what is unnecessary, and identifying what is missing. It is an essential step that helps establish the foundation for developing a more consistent and satisfying personal style.

Planning and Plan Development: Planning and plan development are fundamental stages in image consultation, where the information gathered during the initial meeting and wardrobe analysis is translated into a practical and personalized action plan. This plan is the result of careful consideration of the client's needs, style, and specific goals.

After gaining a clear understanding of the client's current style and areas in need of improvement, the consultant begins to craft a plan that will guide the client through the process of transforming their style and wardrobe. This plan is tailored to each client and can vary significantly based on individual needs.

One of the key elements of the plan is wardrobe review. This may include decisions about which garments to keep, modify, or remove. The consultant can suggest ways to repurpose or revitalize some existing pieces, such as through creative pairings or minor tailoring adjustments.

The purchase of new clothing is another important aspect of the plan. This is not just shopping for the sake of it but a targeted process to fill gaps in the client's wardrobe, taking into account the budget, personal preferences, and style needs. The consultant may accompany the client on shopping trips or provide advice on where to find the most suitable pieces.

Guidance on colors and styles forms a crucial part of the plan. The consultant provides direction on which colors complement the client the most, which styles best suit their body type and personality, and how these can be incorporated into their wardrobe.

Additionally, the plan includes ideas for combining different outfits. The consultant demonstrates how to create various combinations with both existing and new clothing, thus maximizing the versatility of the wardrobe. This can include advice on dressing for different occasions, seasons, and functions, ensuring the client has suitable attire for every aspect of their life.

In conclusion, planning and plan development are carefully curated processes aimed at providing the client with a clear and practical path to achieve their image goals. This phase is a collaboration between consultant and client, where the consultant uses their expertise to guide the client towards a renewed and more authentic image.

Shopping and Garment Selection: Shopping and garment selection are key moments in image consultation, where the recommendations made during the planning phase are put into action. This phase is essential for transforming the client's wardrobe and helping them achieve their style goals.

During shopping, the consultant works closely with the client, providing expert guidance in choosing new clothing. This can happen in various ways. In some cases, the consultant may personally accompany the client to stores, offering immediate advice on fit, style, and color combinations. This personalized shopping experience is particularly helpful as it allows the client to try on clothing and receive real-time feedback.

Alternatively, especially in situations where the client prefers online shopping or has time constraints, the consultant can provide remote assistance. In this scenario, the consultant may preselect a range of items online and send links to the client, or they may consult the client through video calls during online shopping.

Regardless of the mode, shopping is always guided by the client's preferences and the established action plan. The consultant ensures that each purchase aligns with the agreed-upon style goals and fits within the client's budget. The goal is to select clothing that is not only fashionable and affordable for the client but also seamlessly integrates into their existing wardrobe, offering a variety of outfit options.

The consultant also focuses on selecting versatile garments that can be used in different combinations, thereby maximizing the client's investment. A good image consultant considers not only current trends but also the uniqueness of the client's personal style, ensuring that new purchases reflect their personality and enhance their overall image.

In conclusion, shopping and garment selection are personalized and thoughtful steps aimed at creating a wardrobe that is not only aesthetically pleasing but also functional and aligned with the client's lifestyle and needs.

Fittings and Adjustments: Fittings and adjustments are important phases in image consultation, especially when introducing new garments into the client's wardrobe. Even the most beautiful garment may not have the desired effect if it doesn't fit the client properly. That's why the fitting and modification process is crucial to ensure that every new purchase enhances the client's appearance to the fullest.

After shopping, the image consultant ensures that all new garments are tried on by the client. This is the moment when the fit of each piece is carefully evaluated. The consultant examines aspects such as sleeve length, fit around the bust, hips, and waist, and the overall length of the garments. Details like how a garment drapes or moves on the body are also considered, as they can significantly impact the overall look.

If during fittings it's discovered that some garments require modifications for a perfect fit, the consultant can guide the client through the tailoring process. This may include sending the garments to a trusted tailor for adjustments such as taking in or letting out a dress, shortening jacket sleeves, or altering the hem of a pair of pants.

The consultant can also provide suggestions on how garments can be modified to better suit the client's style and preferences. For example, a dress can be transformed by adding or removing details, changing buttons, or adding accessories like belts or pins to further personalize it.

Furthermore, the consultant assists the client in understanding what types of modifications are possible and realistic, helping them make informed decisions about which garments to alter and how. This step ensures that the client not only looks their best in their new clothes but also feels comfortable and confident in them.

In conclusion, fittings and adjustments are essential steps to customize the image consultation process. These phases ensure that each garment not only fits perfectly but is also a true reflection of the client's personal and unique style.

Building and Organizing the Wardrobe: Building and organizing the wardrobe are crucial steps in image consultation. After selecting new garments and making any necessary modifications, the next task is to seamlessly integrate these new acquisitions into the client's existing wardrobe so that everything works harmoniously together. This phase is not just about adding new pieces but also optimizing the entire wardrobe to maximize its functionality and versatility.

The consultant guides the client through the process of organizing the wardrobe in a way that makes it easy to choose outfits every day. This may include grouping similar items together, such as hanging all pants, shirts, or jackets in specific areas, or organizing the wardrobe by color or season. Good organization helps the client see more clearly what they own and makes for quicker and more effective decisions when getting dressed.

Another important aspect is showing the client how to combine the new pieces with existing ones to create versatile outfits. The consultant can create various combinations and demonstrate how the same items can be adapted for different occasions, from work to leisure, from formal events to casual outings. This includes tips on matching colors and fabrics, layering clothing, and using accessories to add interest or change the look of an outfit.

The consultant can also provide practical advice on how to maintain and care for garments so that they remain in good condition for as long as possible. This may include tips on washing and storing different fabrics and how to protect delicate or high-quality items.

Furthermore, building and organizing the wardrobe may involve identifying any remaining gaps. Even after shopping, new needs may arise, and the consultant can suggest further purchases or modifications to truly complete the client's wardrobe.

In conclusion, building and organizing the wardrobe are final steps aimed at ensuring that the client not only has an aesthetically pleasing and up-to-date wardrobe but also that every element is functional and well-integrated, allowing the client to easily create outfits that fit their lifestyle and needs.

Follow-up and Evaluation: After implementing the plan, follow-up meetings are conducted to assess the results and ensure client satisfaction. These meetings are also an opportunity to make any necessary adjustments or modifications.

This process aims not only to improve the client's external image but also to strengthen their confidence and self-esteem, providing them with the tools to best express their personality through style.

DEBUNKING MYTHS: IMAGE CONSULTING IS ONLY FOR WARDROBE RENEWAL

The myth that image consulting is solely focused on wardrobe renewal is a limiting idea that fails to grasp the breadth and depth of what this profession can offer. Image consulting goes far beyond just selecting new clothing; it involves a broader transformation that touches on various aspects of personal image and self-confidence. Here are some clarifications to debunk this myth:

Development of Personal Style: Image consulting is not limited to suggesting new purchases but helps clients develop or refine their personal style. This includes understanding which types of clothing best suit their body type, which color palette enhances their appearance the most, and how to express their personality through clothing.

Self-esteem and Confidence: An important goal of image consulting is to enhance the client's self-esteem and confidence. Seeing oneself in a new light, with clothing that enhances and makes one feel comfortable, can have a profound impact on how a person perceives themselves and interacts with others.

Adapting to Life Changes: Image consulting can be particularly helpful during times of transition or change in a person's life, such as a new job, a change in weight, or a new phase in life. The consultant helps navigate these changes, ensuring that the wardrobe reflects the client's new reality.

Comprehensive Guidance: In addition to clothing, many image consultants provide advice on grooming, makeup, hairstyling, and even body language and etiquette. This holistic approach to personal image helps create a consistent and authentic image.

Continuing Education: Image consulting doesn't end with the purchase of new clothing. It often includes training on how to mix and match outfits, how to organize the wardrobe, and how to make independent style choices in the future.

In conclusion, debunking the myth that image consulting is limited to wardrobe renewal allows us to appreciate the true essence of this profession: helping people feel better about themselves through the expression of their personal style.

THE PERSONAL SHOPPING

Personal Shopping is an increasingly requested and appreciated service that goes beyond the simple act of shopping. It is an art, a science, and a form of consultancy that combines knowledge of fashion, understanding of personal style, and listening skills to create a customized shopping experience for the client. This service is not limited to selecting clothing and accessories; it is a holistic process aimed at understanding and meeting the specific needs of each individual.

The personal shopper works closely with the client to identify their style needs, preferences, and goals, whether they are related to updating their wardrobe, preparing for a special event, or creating an entirely new look. This role requires a mix of skills: a deep knowledge of current trends, an eye for style and quality, and, most importantly, the ability to translate the client's needs and desires into concrete fashion choices.

The personal shopping service stands out for its customization. Each shopping session is designed to be a unique experience tailored to the specific needs of the client. The personal shopper considers factors such as the client's budget, style goals, body type, and the occasions for which they are shopping. Additionally, they provide outfit pairing advice, offering tips on how to combine new purchases with the client's existing wardrobe.

The personal shopper not only facilitates clothing selection but also helps the client make more informed and strategic purchasing decisions. This means choosing garments that not only fit current fashion trends but are also versatile, durable, and suitable for the client's lifestyle and personality. The goal is to build a wardrobe that is not only beautiful and fashionable but also functional and able to withstand the test of time.

In conclusion, Personal Shopping is a service that goes well beyond shopping assistance; it is a personalized experience that transforms the way clients see and experience fashion. It offers an opportunity to explore new styles, experiment with one's image, and, above all, build a wardrobe that truly reflects who they are and how they wish to be perceived by the world.

ORGANIZING A PERSONALIZED SHOPPING SESSION

Organizing a personalized shopping session is a process that requires attention to detail and a deep understanding of the client's needs and desires. This type of shopping is not just a trip to stores; it is a curated experience aimed at making shopping more efficient, enjoyable, and aligned with the client's style goals.

Before planning a personalized shopping session, the personal shopper begins with a thorough discussion with the client. In this initial interview, the client's style preferences, body type, occasions for which they need new clothing, and any specific goals they want to achieve with the shopping session are explored. Budget and any brand or style preferences are also considered.

Based on this information, the personal shopper develops a plan for the shopping session. This may include a selection of stores that fit the client's style and budget, as well as a preliminary list of items or types of clothing to look for. In some cases, the personal shopper may even arrange in advance with the stores, preselecting items for the client to try on.

On the day of shopping, the personal shopper guides the client through a carefully chosen series of stores, ensuring that each stop is in line with the predetermined style goals. During shopping, the personal shopper offers advice on fit, colors, fabrics, and styles, helping the client make choices that not only complement their appearance and preferences but also strategically expand their wardrobe.

An important aspect of a personalized shopping session is education. The personal shopper explains the reasoning behind each choice, helping the client understand which styles work best for them and how to mix the new purchases with items already in their wardrobe. The goal is to provide the client with the tools and knowledge to make independent style choices in the future.

At the end of the session, the client will not only have purchased new clothing but will also have gained increased confidence in their style decisions. The personal shopper can provide a summary of the session, including tips on how to incorporate the new purchases into their existing wardrobe and ideas for future purchases or updates.

In conclusion, a personalized shopping session is much more than just a day of shopping; it is an enriching and educational experience that helps the client build a wardrobe that not only looks exceptional but also reflects their personal style and way of life.

Building a functional wardrobe is an essential process in image consulting and personal shopping that goes beyond simply accumulating fashionable garments. It involves creating a collection of clothes that are not only aesthetically pleasing but also practical, versatile, and suitable for the client's everyday life needs.

A functional wardrobe starts with a solid foundation of essential pieces often referred to as "basics." These include high-quality white shirts, well-tailored pants, a classic jacket, perfectly fitting jeans, and other items that can form the basis for a variety of outfits. These garments should be selected for their quality and versatility so they can easily be combined with other pieces to create different combinations.

Next, the process involves adding items that add personality and style to the wardrobe. These can include trendy pieces, distinctive accessories, vibrant colors, or unique prints. However, it's important that these "character" elements are chosen to integrate well with the basic garments, allowing the client to vary their outfits without having to own an excessive number of items.

The personal shopper or image consultant assists the client in evaluating each item in their existing wardrobe and deciding what to keep, what to alter, and what to eliminate. This includes careful consideration of fit, style, and how often the client wears each item. Items that don't fit well, are outdated, or no longer reflect the client's personal style can be removed, making space for new purchases that align with their current image.

Functionality also involves wardrobe organization. A well-organized wardrobe, where each garment is easily visible and accessible, makes it easier for the client to choose outfits and mix and match items. The personal shopper can provide advice on how to physically organize clothes, such as grouping them by type, color, or season.

Finally, a crucial aspect of building a functional wardrobe is adaptability. This means having garments that can be easily adapted for different contexts, seasons, or occasions. For example, a dress can be worn with a blazer for a professional look or with statement jewelry for an elegant evening ensemble.

In summary, building a functional wardrobe means creating a collection of clothes that the client loves to wear, that suits their daily activities, and that can be easily mixed and matched to create a variety of attractive outfits consistent with their personal image.

FREQUENTLY ASKED QUESTIONS: HOW CAN I OPTIMIZE MY SHOPPING EXPERIENCE?

Optimizing your shopping is a common goal for many people looking to make their shopping sessions more efficient, targeted, and satisfying. Here are some tips that can help streamline the shopping process:

Plan Ahead: Before you go shopping, take a moment to plan. Consider what clothing items you truly need, what gaps exist in your wardrobe, and what your style goals are. Making a list can help you stay focused while shopping.

Know Your Style and Measurements: Having a good understanding of your personal style and your measurements can make shopping much more efficient. This helps you quickly filter out items that don't fit your style or size.

Set a Budget: Establishing a budget before you go shopping can help avoid impulse purchases and focus on what you truly need. It also helps make more conscious decisions about which items are worth investing more in.

Quality Over Quantity: Prefer quality over quantity. Buying fewer high-quality items that last longer and fit better is more beneficial than accumulating many cheap and low-quality items.

Research Brands and Collections: Before you go shopping, research current brands and collections. This helps you know what to expect and which stores to visit to find what you're looking for.

Always Try On Clothing: Make sure to try on clothing before purchasing. Even if you know your size, measurements can vary depending on the brand and style. Trying on clothes ensures they fit well and are comfortable.

Be Selective: Don't be afraid to be selective. If a clothing item doesn't fully convince you, it's probably not a good choice. Listen to your instincts and choose only items that genuinely excite you.

Consider Versatility: When buying a new item, think about how it will integrate into your existing wardrobe. Consider whether you can easily pair it with at least three different outfits.

Conscious Shopping: Be mindful of your shopping habits and try to avoid impulse purchases. Take the time to reflect on each purchase and how it fits into your lifestyle and wardrobe.

Seek Guidance If Necessary: If you have difficulty making decisions or finding what you need, don't hesitate to seek help from an image consultant or personal shopper. They can offer valuable guidance and help you make more targeted choices.

By following these tips, you can transform your shopping into a more targeted, enjoyable, and productive experience, ensuring that you add clothing items to your wardrobe that you truly love and that complement your personal style.

MYTHS TO DEBUNK: PERSONAL SHOPPING IS ALWAYS EXPENSIVE

The myth that personal shopping is always expensive is a common belief that doesn't necessarily reflect reality. Personal shopping is an accessible and flexible service designed to fit a wide range of budgets and needs. Here are some key points that debunk this myth:

Customizable Services: Personal shoppers offer a variety of services that can be tailored to fit different budgets. This ranges from basic consulting, such as helping with the selection of specific items, to a full wardrobe makeover service. Clients have the flexibility to choose the level of service that best suits their financial needs.

Long-Term Investment: Using the services of a personal shopper can be a smart investment. By helping to select quality and versatile clothing, the personal shopper can help reduce impulsive or impractical purchases. This means less waste and a more functional and durable wardrobe.

Access to a Range of Prices: Personal shoppers are not limited to high-end or luxury stores. They are experts at finding the best value for every budget and often know about the best deals and discounts available, both in physical stores and online.

Time and Energy Savings: Personal shopping is also a time and energy saver. For those with a busy lifestyle, the efficiency of having someone research and select the right items can be invaluable.

Not Just for Luxury Items: Many personal shoppers work with a variety of brands and styles, not exclusively luxury items. Their main goal is to find the best style for the client, regardless of the price of the clothing.

Added Value: In addition to finding clothing, personal shoppers offer added value in terms of style advice, helping to build a personal image that reflects the client's personality and lifestyle.

In conclusion, personal shopping is a versatile service that can be adapted to fit a variety of budgets and preferences. It is not exclusively a luxury for a few, but a useful and accessible tool for anyone looking to improve their style and optimize their wardrobe.

WARDROBE ANALYSIS

"Wardrobe Analysis" is a fundamental process in image consulting, as it provides a detailed overview of the client's current style and areas that can be improved or updated. This phase is not just an opportunity to tidy up but an exercise to better understand one's style, what works, and what no longer works in the current context of the client's life.

During the wardrobe analysis, the image consultant works together with the client to examine every item present in their closet. This includes not only clothing but also accessories, shoes, and even underwear and sleepwear. The goal is to assess each piece for its style, condition, fit, and how often it is actually worn.

A key step is to identify the items that the client loves and that make them feel comfortable and confident. These pieces often reflect the client's true style and can serve as a foundation for building the rest of the wardrobe. At the same time, items that are no longer suitable, both in terms of style and fit, are identified, and decisions are made whether to alter, donate, or eliminate them.

During the analysis, consideration is also given to the items that are missing in the wardrobe and that could enhance its versatility. Perhaps the client needs more basic pieces or some key items that can elevate their style. The analysis helps create a targeted shopping list that addresses specific style and functionality needs, rather than impulsive or random purchases.

Wardrobe analysis is also a time to discuss closet organization. A well-organized wardrobe helps the client see clearly what they own, making it easier to choose daily outfits. The consultant can provide tips on how to organize items by type, color, or frequency of use.

In conclusion, wardrobe analysis is not just a practical exercise but also an opportunity to reflect on one's personal style and how it fits with their current lifestyle and aspirations. It is a fundamental step towards building a wardrobe that not only looks exceptional but also reflects the client's authentic and desired personal image.

HOW TO CONDUCT AN EFFECTIVE WARDROBE ANALYSIS

Conducting an Effective Wardrobe Analysis is a process that requires attention and consideration, as it involves evaluating not only the clothing items but also the client's lifestyle and personal preferences. This process helps create a wardrobe that is functional, representative of personal style, and tailored to daily needs.

Beginning the wardrobe analysis starts with a general observation of the existing clothing. This means considering every item, from basic pieces like pants and shirts to accessories, shoes, and even special occasion garments. The key is to assess each piece not only for its appearance but also how frequently it is worn and its versatility.

The first step may be to categorize the wardrobe into sections. Sorting items by type and season can help visualize what one owns and identify any gaps. For example, one might discover having many winter garments but few for summer, or an abundance of formal attire but a lack of casual options.

Next, the fit and condition of each garment are examined. Clothes that do not fit properly, are worn out, or no longer reflect current taste can be set aside. This phase is also an opportunity to consider sartorial alterations that could breathe new life into otherwise unused items.

Another important aspect is assessing the color and style of each garment. Consider how colors complement the client's complexion and whether the styles reflect their personality and lifestyle. Understanding which colors and styles work best can guide future purchasing decisions.

The analysis also includes a discussion of the client's style preferences. This helps understand which types of clothing they feel most comfortable wearing and which they avoid. Lifestyle habits, such as the type of work, leisure activities, and social needs, are considered to ensure the wardrobe aligns with the client's daily life.

Finally, a list is created of what is missing from the wardrobe. This could include basic pieces, versatile items that can be mixed and matched in various ways, or even some trendy pieces to update the style. The goal is to ensure that, by the end of the analysis, the client has a clear path toward a wardrobe that is not only aesthetically pleasing but also fully functional for their needs.

In summary, an effective wardrobe analysis is not just a process of reviewing and organizing but a thorough assessment that considers fit, style, color, and functionality, resulting in a wardrobe that truly reflects the client's personal style and life.

FREQUENTLY ASKED QUESTIONS: WHEN IS IT TIME TO REFRESH THE WARDROBE?

A frequently asked question that many people have is when is the right time to refresh their wardrobe. The decision to refresh the wardrobe can depend on various factors, and there is no one-size-fits-all answer. Here are some signs that may indicate it's time to consider a wardrobe update:

1. **Life or Lifestyle Changes**: Significant life changes, such as a new job, weight fluctuations, or alterations in daily routines, may call for a wardrobe update. For example, transitioning from a casual work environment to a formal one may require a different type of clothing.

2. **Ill-Fitting Clothes**: If many of your garments no longer fit properly due to changes in weight or natural wear and tear, it may be time to refresh certain parts of your wardrobe.

3. **Outdated or Unrepresentative Style**: If you find that your wardrobe no longer reflects your current taste or who you are today, it might be time for an update. Personal style can evolve over time, and your wardrobe should evolve with you.

4. **Difficulty Choosing What to Wear**: If you often struggle to decide what to wear despite having a full wardrobe, it could be a sign that many pieces no longer meet your needs or preferences.

5. **Worn-Out or Damaged Items**: Garments that are visibly worn, faded, or damaged should be replaced. A well-maintained wardrobe is a key element for a polished and professional

appearance.

6. **Lack of Versatility**: If your current wardrobe doesn't offer enough versatility to mix and match and create different outfits for various occasions, it may be time to add more versatile pieces.

7. **Desire for a Refresh**: Sometimes, the desire to refresh the wardrobe simply stems from the willingness to change and experiment with new styles, colors, or trends.

Refreshing the wardrobe doesn't necessarily mean replacing every item; it can be a gradual process where you gradually introduce new pieces while phasing out old or no longer suitable ones. The goal should be to have a wardrobe that makes you feel confident, comfortable, and representative of your personal style.

MYTHS TO DEBUNK: ONE MUST ALWAYS FOLLOW THE LATEST TRENDS

The myth that one must always follow the latest fashion trends is a fairly common belief, but not necessarily true or beneficial for everyone. While trends can provide inspiration and fresh ideas, blindly following every new fashion trend may not always be the best choice for developing a distinctive and long-lasting personal style. Here are some reasons why it's not essential to always follow the latest trends:

Individual Style: Everyone has their own unique style that expresses their personality and lifestyle. Following every new trend can lead to a wardrobe that feels disconnected and unrepresentative of one's true self.

Sustainability and Awareness: Constantly buying trendy clothing can contribute to a cycle of excessive and unsustainable consumption. Instead, choosing clothing that is genuinely loved and will last over time can be a more environmentally friendly and mindful approach to fashion.

Budget and Investments: Keeping up with all the latest trends can be expensive. Investing in quality, classic, and versatile pieces that stand the test of time can be a wiser financial choice.

Fit and Comfort: Not all trends are suitable for every body type or comfortable to wear. It's important to choose clothing that fits well and feels comfortable.

Longevity: Fashion is cyclical, and trends come and go. Focusing on a personal style rather than trying to keep up with every trend ensures that the wardrobe remains relevant and loved even as trends change.

In conclusion, while trends can be fun to explore and can offer new insights into one's style, it's neither necessary nor practical to adopt them all. A balanced approach could be to incorporate trend elements that truly resonate with one's personal style while maintaining a core of classic and timeless pieces.

CAMOUFLAGE TECHNIQUES

Camouflage techniques in the realm of fashion and personal style are strategies used to enhance a client's figure by playing to their strengths while minimizing areas they may want to de-emphasize. These techniques go beyond simply hiding or covering up but rather focus on creating visual balance and accentuating the client's best attributes.

Camouflage in clothing relies on the clever use of colors, fabrics, cuts, and patterns to influence how the figure is perceived. For example, using dark colors in specific areas can create the illusion of a slimmer silhouette, while light or bright colors can draw attention to desired points.

The lines and cuts of garments also play a crucial role in camouflage. Vertical lines, for instance, can elongate and slim the figure, while horizontal lines can have the opposite effect. Garment cuts can be used to accentuate or conceal different parts of the body. For instance, an empire-cut dress can emphasize the bust while gently floating over the abdomen.

Another aspect of camouflage involves fabric selection. Fabrics that drape fluidly can mask areas the client prefers not to highlight, whereas more structured fabrics can provide support and definition.

Accessories are also important in camouflage techniques. For instance, a scarf or necklace can be used to draw attention to the face, while a belt can be used to define the waist.

It's essential to emphasize that camouflage techniques are not about masking the client or hiding flaws. Instead, they celebrate and enhance every figure, helping the client feel confident and comfortable in their own style. These techniques are personalized based on the client's individual needs, body type, and personal style goals.

In conclusion, camouflage techniques are a powerful tool in image consulting, used to help clients create an image that reflects their personality and makes them feel their best, regardless of their body shape or size.

CLOTHING TECHNIQUES TO ENHANCE THE FIGURE

Clothing techniques to enhance the figure are fundamental tools for enhancing one's physical appearance and boosting self-confidence through thoughtful fashion choices. These techniques focus on how to use clothing, colors, fabrics, and accessories to create a visually harmonious effect, emphasizing strengths and minimizing areas that the client may want to de-emphasize.

The choice of colors plays a significant role in this process. For example, darker colors tend to have a slimming effect and can be used to minimize specific areas of the body, while bright colors or patterns can draw attention to areas you want to emphasize. Using color contrast can help direct the gaze to the body's strong points.

The cuts and lines of clothing are equally important. Vertical lines, for example, can create a slimming and elongating effect, while horizontal lines can widen. Garments with specific cuts can accentuate or conceal different parts of the body, such as a fitted waist dress to emphasize an hourglass figure or an A-line cut to minimize hips.

Fabric choice is crucial for how a garment drapes and fits the body. Light and fluid fabrics can conceal and minimize, while more structured ones can provide support and definition. Playing with textures can add visual interest and help balance the figure.

Accessories, such as belts, jewelry, or scarves, can be used strategically to draw attention to specific areas of the body or add a focal point that diverts attention from other areas.

Balancing proportions is essential to creating a harmonious look. This means balancing the upper and lower parts of the body, for example, using dark colors on areas you want to minimize and lighter or brighter tones on the parts of the body you want to emphasize.

Finally, it is essential that all these techniques align with the client's personal style. The goal is to enhance the figure without compromising personal expression and comfort. Clothing techniques to enhance the figure should never feel restrictive but rather be tools to help the client feel confident and comfortable with their appearance.

FREQUENTLY ASKED QUESTIONS: WHAT ARE CAMOUFLAGE TECHNIQUES?

Camouflage techniques in the field of fashion and personal style are methods used to enhance a person's physical appearance by emphasizing their strengths and minimizing areas they may want to de-emphasize. These techniques aim not to "hide" the body but rather to create a visual balance that enhances the overall figure.

The concept of camouflage in clothing is based on a detailed understanding of how specific style choices can influence the perception of the body. This approach involves not just hiding or covering but strategically using colors, clothing cuts, fabrics, and patterns.

The use of colors plays a fundamental role in this process. Dark colors, such as black, navy blue, or dark brown, are known for their slimming effect as they tend to absorb light rather than reflect it. This can create the illusion of a slimmer and more tapered silhouette. On the other hand, bright or vibrant colors like white, yellow, or red can capture attention and highlight areas of the body where they are applied. The strategic use of these colors can help emphasize strengths and divert attention from areas the client wishes to minimize.

The clothing cuts also play a crucial role in camouflage. For example, dresses that emphasize the waist can create a more proportionate look, especially for those with an hourglass figure. For more rectangular figures, garments that create the illusion of curves, such as those with peplum, can be flattering. Vertical cuts, like those in some coats or jackets, can elongate the figure, while horizontal cuts can widen it.

The choice of fabrics is equally important. Lightweight and flowing fabrics can conceal and minimize, creating an illusion of fluidity and lightness. Conversely, heavier and structured fabrics can provide definition and support where needed.

Additionally, patterns and prints play a significant role in camouflage. Bold and large patterns can attract attention and are ideal for areas of the body that you want to emphasize. Small and subtle patterns, on the other hand, tend to be more discreet and can be used for areas you want to minimize.

In summary, clothing camouflage is an art that involves balancing and combining various elements to best enhance the figure. This process goes beyond simply selecting garments; it's about a deep understanding of how different elements of clothing can work together to create a coherent and harmonious image, thereby boosting the client's confidence and self-image.

Clothing cuts play a fundamental role in camouflage. For example, dresses with vertical lines can elongate and slim the figure, while those with horizontal lines or large prints can have the opposite effect. Specific cuts can also help highlight certain parts of the body, such as an empire cut to emphasize the bust or an A-line skirt to balance broad shoulders.

The choice of fabrics is equally important. Fabrics that drape fluidly can conceal areas you want to de-emphasize, creating the illusion of fluidity and lightness. Conversely, more structured fabrics can provide definition and support.

Accessories can be used strategically in the camouflage process. For example, a long, flowing scarf can divert attention from other areas of the body, while a strategically placed belt can help define the waist.

In conclusion, camouflage techniques are a sophisticated aspect of image consulting and personal style that require a deep understanding of how different fashion elements can be combined to best enhance a person's figure. These techniques allow those who use them to feel more confident and comfortable in their bodies, regardless of their shape or size.

DEBUNKING MYTHS: CAMOUFLAGE IS ONLY FOR HIDING FLAWS

The myth that camouflage in clothing is used solely to conceal flaws is a limited and restrictive conception of this technique. In reality, camouflage is much more: it is a sophisticated method for enhancing one's figure, boosting self-confidence, and expressing personal style. Here are some clarifications to debunk this myth:

Enhancement Rather than Concealment: The true aim of camouflage is not to hide so-called "flaws" but rather to highlight strengths and create visual balance. This can mean emphasizing a person's best features while minimizing areas that might make them feel less confident.

Expression of Personal Style: Camouflage is also a tool for expressing personal style. The use of specific colors, cuts, and fabrics allows individuals to emphasize their personal taste and uniqueness through clothing.

Improving Proportion and Balance: Camouflage techniques can be used to create balance in body proportions. For example, they can help balance an inverted triangle figure or enhance an hourglass silhouette.

Boosting Confidence: Effective use of camouflage helps people feel more confident in their appearance. When wearing clothing that enhances their figure, it can have a significant impact on self-confidence and self-esteem.

Adaptability to Every Body Type: Camouflage is not a technique reserved only for certain body types or sizes; it is adaptable to anyone. Regardless of shape or size, camouflage techniques can be used to enhance every figure.

Art and Creativity: Using camouflage techniques requires creativity and an artistic eye. It involves skillfully combining different design elements to create a look that is not only flattering but also aesthetically pleasing.

In conclusion, camouflage in clothing is an art that goes far beyond merely concealing flaws. It is a powerful tool for enhancing the body, expressing one's style identity, and walking with greater confidence and self-assurance.

CLIENTS

In the profession of personal shopping and image consulting, understanding and meeting the needs of various types of clients is fundamental. Each client comes with a unique set of expectations, preferences, and style challenges, making customization of services not only essential but also one of the most rewarding aspects of the job.

The diversity of clients in this field is wide-ranging: some may be looking for a complete wardrobe overhaul, while others may need assistance for a specific event. Some clients are well-informed about fashion trends and wish to incorporate them into their style, while others may be less focused on trends and more interested in finding a style that reflects their personality and lifestyle.

The first step in working with each new client is to understand who they are and what they are looking for. This can be achieved through initial discussions, questionnaires, and in some cases, a review of their current wardrobe. These tools help identify the client's style, preferences, body type, and areas they wish to focus on.

Customizing the service requires a flexible approach. For example, a client who prefers a classic and timeless look will require a different approach than someone who is enthusiastic about experimenting with the latest trends. For some clients, factors like practicality and comfort may be important, especially if they have an active lifestyle or specific needs related to their work or personal environment.

Additionally, developing open and honest communication with clients is essential. Actively listening to and addressing their concerns not only helps build trust but also provides valuable insights that can guide the consulting process. It's important for the client to feel heard, understood, and respected in their style choices.

In conclusion, customizing services in personal shopping and image consulting is crucial to cater to a variety of clients with different needs and tastes. Understanding and respecting each client's uniqueness, along with effective communication and adaptability, are the keys to providing a service that is both satisfying and transformative for the client.

TYPES OF CLIENTS AND CUSTOMIZATION OF SERVICES

In the field of personal shopping and image consulting, the variety of client types is broad and diverse. Each client brings a unique set of needs, preferences, and style goals, making customization of the service not only necessary but also an essential part of the job. The ability to recognize and adapt to different needs is crucial for providing quality service.

Some clients may be looking for a complete wardrobe makeover. These clients may have undergone significant life changes, such as a new career or a weight change, and need assistance in reflecting these changes in their style. Others may seek assistance for specific events, such as weddings, job interviews, or other important occasions.

There are also clients who approach personal shopping services with the goal of exploring new trends or experimenting with their personal style. These clients are often open to experimentation and seek advice on incorporating current fashion elements into their wardrobe without losing their style identity.

On the other hand, some clients may be less interested in trends and more focused on finding a style that reflects their personality and daily needs. These clients value functionality, comfort, and the longevity of garments and seek versatile pieces that can be easily integrated into their existing wardrobe.

For each type of client, it is essential to establish clear and open communication. Listening carefully to their preferences, concerns, and goals helps build a tailored action plan. It is important to show empathy and understanding while providing expert guidance and useful advice.

Customization can include selecting specific garments, advising on combinations and pairings, assisting in the purchase of specific items, or guiding the creation of an entirely new wardrobe. The personal shopper or image consultant must be flexible and adaptable, capable of providing creative solutions that respect the client's tastes and life needs, regardless of their personal style or lifestyle.

In conclusion, the variety of client types in personal shopping and image consulting requires a personalized and attentive approach. Understanding the unique needs of each client and adapting services to meet those needs is essential to ensure that each client receives the attention and care they deserve.

FREQUENTLY ASKED QUESTIONS: HOW TO HANDLE CLIENTS WITH DIFFERENT TASTES?

Managing clients with different tastes is a common but stimulating challenge in the world of personal shopping and image consulting. Each client has unique preferences and an individual sense of style, which requires a flexible and personalized approach. Here are some strategies for effectively handling clients with different tastes:

Active Listening: The key to managing clients with different tastes is to listen actively. Take the time to understand their preferences, lifestyles, and what they are looking for in their wardrobe. This not only shows respect for their needs but also provides valuable information to guide your recommendations.

Empathy and Open-Mindedness: Being empathetic and maintaining an open mind are essential. Even if the client's tastes differ from yours or from what you would normally recommend, it's important to respect their choices and work within their comfort parameters.

Education and Guidance: Provide education and guidance where necessary. Some clients may not be aware of how certain styles or cuts can enhance their appearance. Your expertise can help them explore new options they might love but have never considered.

Personalization of Service: Tailor your services to each client's individual tastes. This may include selecting stores, brands, styles, and fabrics that align with their personal preferences.

Flexibility and Creativity: Use your flexibility and creativity to find solutions that satisfy different tastes. This may involve blending elements from different styles or finding a balance between what the client wants and what works for their body shape and lifestyle.

Building Trust: Demonstrate your reliability and expertise through thoughtful suggestions and well-justified choices. When clients see that your recommendations enhance their appearance and align with their tastes, they are more likely to trust your decisions.

Ongoing Feedback: Seek regular feedback and be willing to make adjustments based on their responses. This process of mutual learning helps refine the service you provide and enhances client satisfaction.

Respect for Individual Choices: Finally, it is essential to respect individual choices. Each client is unique, and their style should reflect their personality, not a standard formula.

Managing clients with different tastes requires patience, understanding, and a good dose of creativity. Your role is to help each client feel their best in their own style, regardless of how much their preferences may vary.

MYTHS TO DEBUNK: ALL CLIENTS WANT TO FOLLOW FASHION

The myth that all clients want to follow fashion is a common belief, but it doesn't accurately reflect the reality of image consulting and personal shopping. The truth is that clients' tastes and needs are incredibly diverse, and not everyone is interested in blindly following the latest fashion trends. Here are some reasons why this myth doesn't hold up:

Diverse Priorities: Many clients aim to express their individual sense of style rather than blindly following trends. These clients prioritize personal expression, comfort, and functionality in clothing over simply adhering to the latest fashions.

Unique Personal Style: Each client has a unique sense of style that often transcends current fashion trends. What works for one person in terms of style, color, and fit may not be suitable for another. Many clients are looking for a look that reflects their personality and lifestyle.

Practical Considerations: For some clients, practical considerations like budget, comfort, and versatility are more important than the latest trends. These clients prefer to invest in timeless, quality pieces that will last for seasons to come.

Self-Representation: Many clients are more interested in finding a way to represent themselves and their values through clothing rather than conforming to an image dictated by current fashion. This can include adopting a style that reflects their ethical beliefs, such as sustainable fashion or veganism.

Generational and Cultural Differences: Style preferences can vary significantly depending on age, culture, and the client's background. Not all demographic groups identify with prevailing fashion trends, and many may have an entirely different view of what is fashionable or desirable.

In summary, debunking the myth that all clients want to follow fashion is important to understand the diversity of needs and expectations in personal shopping and image consulting. Recognizing and respecting clients' individual preferences is crucial for providing a service that is truly personalized and reflects their unique sense of style.

HOW TO BUILD YOUR CAREER

Creating a successful career as a personal shopper or image consultant is a journey that requires dedication, a passion for fashion, and a deep understanding of clients' needs. Starting in the field goes beyond knowing the latest trends; it also involves developing a set of key skills and competencies.

Training and education are the crucial initial steps. This may involve pursuing formal studies in fashion, design, or communication, as well as attending specific courses or obtaining certifications in personal shopping and image consulting. These programs offer a solid foundation of technical and theoretical knowledge and can provide valuable insights into the industry.

Gaining practical experience is equally important. Working in boutiques, department stores, or for fashion brands can offer hands-on experience and an inside look at how the industry operates. It's also an excellent opportunity to build a professional network and begin developing your own consulting style.

A portfolio showcasing your work and successes can serve as a powerful marketing tool. Including examples of style transformations you've achieved, outfits you've created, and any other work that highlights your skills and unique style is essential for attracting new clients.

Building a strong network of contacts and collaborations is crucial. Participating in fashion events, fairs, and workshops can not only provide additional knowledge but also opportunities to meet potential clients or collaborators. Collaborating with photographers, stylists, and influencers can increase your visibility and open new doors.

Staying up-to-date with the latest trends and dynamics in the fashion market is fundamental. This knowledge allows you to provide current and relevant consultations, increasing client trust and satisfaction.

Marketing and personal promotion are essential to growing your career. Developing a strong online presence through social media, a website, or a blog can help showcase your work and reach a wider audience. Sharing style tips, trends, and image transformations can draw attention to you as an expert in the field.

Providing excellent customer service is the heart of your business. Carefully listening to your clients, addressing their needs, and exceeding their expectations will not only make them more satisfied but can also lead to recommendations and positive reviews, essential for your success.

Lastly, being adaptable and committed to continuous learning is vital in an ever-evolving industry. Attending refresher courses, reading industry magazines, and staying open to new ideas and trends will keep you current and ensure your services remain relevant and sought-after.

In summary, developing a successful career in personal shopping and image consulting requires a blend of education, experience, networking, marketing, excellent customer service, and a constant commitment to learning and adaptability. With these foundations, you can build a rewarding career that not only fulfills your passion for fashion but also allows you to have a significant impact on your clients' style and confidence.

TIPS FOR STARTING AND GROWING PROFESSIONALLY

Starting and growing professionally in the field of personal shopping and image consulting requires more than a passion for fashion; it's a process that involves building a strong foundation of knowledge, developing a network of contacts, and a commitment to continuous personal and professional growth. Here are some tips on how to start and grow in this dynamic and rewarding field.

First and foremost, education is crucial. Consider pursuing studies in relevant fields such as fashion, design, marketing, or communication. Specialized courses or certifications in personal shopping and image consulting can provide a solid foundation of theoretical and practical knowledge and an introduction to the industry.

Gaining practical experience is equally important. You may start with internships or entry-level positions in boutiques, department stores, or fashion companies. This hands-on experience not only provides a practical understanding of the industry but also offers the opportunity to build a professional network and develop practical skills.

A strong portfolio is a powerful marketing tool. Include examples of style transformations you have achieved, outfits you have created, and any other work that demonstrates your skills and unique style. A well-curated portfolio can attract new clients and showcase your expertise.

Building a network of contacts is essential. Attend fashion events, fairs, and workshops to meet other industry professionals and potential clients. Collaborating with photographers, stylists, and influencers can also increase your visibility and open up new opportunities.

Staying up-to-date on the latest trends and dynamics in the fashion market is essential. This allows you to offer up-to-date and relevant consultations, increasing the trust and satisfaction of your clients.

Developing a strong online presence through social media, a personal website, or a blog can help showcase your work to a wider audience. Sharing style tips, trends, and image transformations can draw attention to you as an industry expert.

Excellent customer service is at the core of everything. Listen carefully to your clients and exceed their expectations. Quality customer service can lead to recommendations and positive reviews, crucial for your success in the industry.

Finally, continuous learning is vital in a rapidly evolving industry. Stay flexible and committed to developing your skills and knowledge. Attend refresher courses, read industry magazines, and remain open to new ideas and trends.

In conclusion, starting and growing in personal shopping and image consulting requires dedication, education, practical experience, networking skills, a creative marketing approach, excellent customer service, and a commitment to continuous learning and adaptability. With these elements, you can build a rewarding career that satisfies your passion for fashion and allows you to have a positive impact on your clients' style and confidence.

FREQUENTLY ASKED QUESTIONS: WHAT ARE THE FIRST STEPS TO BECOME A PERSONAL SHOPPER?

Becoming a personal shopper is an exciting journey that requires a passion for fashion, excellent interpersonal skills, and a constant commitment to professional development. If you're considering pursuing this career, here are some fundamental steps to follow.

First and foremost, it's essential to have a solid understanding of fashion and its trends. This can be achieved through formal education, such as fashion, design, or marketing courses, or by attending seminars and workshops specific to personal shopping and image consulting. These courses not only provide a theoretical foundation but often offer practical experiences as well.

A crucial aspect is gaining practical experience. You could start by working in clothing stores, boutiques, or department stores. This will give you a firsthand insight into the retail industry's operations and allow you to develop key skills such as customer interaction, understanding their needs, and the ability to make effective style recommendations.

Building a strong portfolio is another important step. As you gain experience, collect examples of looks you've created, customer feedback, and any other materials that showcase your skills and unique style. A well-curated portfolio is essential for showcasing your work to potential clients or employers.

Developing a professional network is crucial. Participating in fashion events, trade shows, and other industry gatherings can help you build relationships with other professionals in the field. These connections can be valuable for finding job opportunities, collaborations, and staying updated on industry trends.

Stay informed about the latest fashion trends and market dynamics. This will enable you to offer current and relevant consultations to your clients. Being a trend expert will also help you build credibility as a personal shopper.

Another important aspect is developing your marketing and promotional skills. In an era dominated by digital media, having a strong online presence through social media, a personal website, or a blog is crucial. These tools can help you reach a wider audience, showcase your work, and attract new clients.

Finally, providing exceptional customer service is vital. Your goal should be not only to help clients find clothing and accessories they love but also to provide a positive and memorable shopping experience. Customer satisfaction will lead to recommendations and loyal clientele.

In conclusion, becoming a personal shopper requires a combination of education, practical experience, networking, and marketing skills, along with a commitment to delivering high-quality customer service. With passion, dedication, and ongoing skill development, you can build a rewarding career helping others feel confident and stylish.

DEBUNKING MYTHS: IT'S DIFFICULT TO SUCCEED AS AN IMAGE CONSULTANT

The career of an image consultant is often surrounded by many myths and misconceptions, one of the most common being the perceived difficulty of achieving success in this field. However, with the right combination of skills, strategy, and determination, becoming a successful image consultant is an achievable and rewarding goal. Let's take a closer look at some crucial aspects to debunk this myth.

Training and Skills: Success begins with a solid foundation of knowledge. An image consultant must have a deep understanding of fashion, style, color theory, and the psychology of clothing. Specialized courses, workshops, and ongoing training are essential to stay updated on the latest trends and techniques.

Interpersonal Skills: The ability to build trusting relationships with clients is essential. Listening, understanding, and responding to their needs, desires, and insecurities are crucial. An effective consultant doesn't just sell a service; they provide a personalized experience that empowers the client.

Personal Brand Development: Creating a personal brand helps distinguish oneself in the market. This includes building a portfolio, a social media presence, networking, and gathering testimonials from satisfied clients. A strong personal brand attracts new clients and creates business opportunities.

Adaptability and Innovation: The world of fashion is constantly evolving, and an image consultant must be able to adapt quickly to changes. Innovation in the services offered and the ability to anticipate or adapt to new trends are key elements in keeping one's offering relevant and appealing.

Marketing and Promotion: Knowing how to market one's services is crucial. This includes the ability to identify and reach the target market, effectively use social media and online platforms to promote the business, and build strategic partnerships.

Feedback and Continuous Improvement: Success is an ongoing process. Gathering feedback from clients and constantly improving the services offered is essential for professional growth and maintaining a high level of customer satisfaction.

Resilience and Determination: Like in any career, there will be challenges and obstacles to overcome. Resilience and determination are indispensable qualities for overcoming difficult times and pursuing one's goals.

In conclusion, becoming a successful image consultant requires more than just a passion for fashion. It is the result of a combination of skills, strategies, and personal qualities. With the right approach, success in this field is not only possible but can also be an extremely gratifying and enriching experience.

FASHION DICTIONARY PART 1 AND PART 2

This section of the book, 'Fashion Dictionary Part 1' and 'Fashion Dictionary Part 2,' is dedicated to providing a detailed and comprehensive glossary of key terms in the world of fashion and personal shopping. The division into two parts allows for organizing and presenting the terms in a clearer and more accessible manner.

Fashion Dictionary Part 1

The first part of the glossary focuses on the fundamental terms in the world of fashion and personal shopping. This section is ideal for readers who are approaching this field for the first time or for those who desire a basic understanding of common terms. It covers:

Basic Terminology: Introduces the most common terms related to types of clothing, cuts, styles, and trends. This includes basic definitions such as "A-line," "empire waist," "peplum," etc.

Types of Fabrics and Materials: Provides an overview of the different fabrics used in fashion, explaining their characteristics, uses, and how they influence the style and comfort of garments.

Design Elements: Includes terms related to various design elements, such as "draping," "lace," "embroidery," providing an understanding of how these details can transform a piece of clothing.

Accessories and Additions: Explores specific terms related to accessories, essential for completing any outfit and for personal shopping consultations.

Fashion Dictionary Part 2

The second part of the glossary delves into more advanced and specific terms, useful for those who already have a basic knowledge of the industry and want to further deepen their understanding:

Advanced and Technical Terminology: Focuses on more technical and specific industry terms, useful for understanding the complexities of fashion design and production.

Historical Styles and Movements: Introduces terms related to important historical styles and movements in fashion, helping to understand how these influence current trends.

Emerging Trends and Contemporary Terminology: Covers the latest trends and emerging language in the world of fashion, essential for staying updated and relevant in the industry.

Personal Shopping Terminology: Explores specific terms related to the personal shopping service, including aspects such as client assessment, wardrobe building, and style consulting.

FASHION AND PERSONAL SHOPPING TERMINOLOGY

First Part

Basic Terminology

A-Line: A dress or skirt silhouette that is narrower at the top and gradually widens towards the hem, creating a shape similar to the letter "A." This style is versatile and flattering for various body types.

Empire Waist: A design where the waistline is raised above the natural waist, often just below the bust. This style emphasizes the upper body and is particularly suitable for dresses and tops.

Peplum: An additional hem or layer of fabric attached to the waist of a garment, creating an overlapping effect that can help define the waist.

Types of Fabrics and Materials

Cashmere: A luxurious fabric obtained from Cashmere goats' wool. It is renowned for its softness, lightweight feel, and warmth.

Chiffon: Lightweight and transparent fabric, made from silk or synthetic fibers. It is loved for its elegance and fluidity, often used in evening dresses and scarves.

Denim: A sturdy cotton fabric with a twill weave, commonly used for jeans and casual jackets.

Design Elements

Draping: A design technique where fabric is arranged in soft folds or cascades, often used to add an elegant touch to clothing.

Lace: Decorative fabric made from intertwined threads in complex patterns. It is often used as a decorative detail on clothing and lingerie.

Embroidery: The art of decorating fabric with a needle and thread, creating designs and patterns. Embroidery can range from simple accents to intricate designs on clothing and accessories.

Accessories and Additions

Fedora: A classic hat with a medium brim and an indented crown. Originally a men's accessory, it is now popular in both male and female styles.

Clutch: A small handbag without handles, often used for formal occasions or evenings out.

Statement Jewelry: Jewelry that grabs attention, characterized by large sizes, vibrant colors, or bold designs. They are used to add a focal point to an outfit.

This glossary serves as a foundation for understanding the most common terms and expressions in the world of fashion and personal shopping, providing aspiring image consultants and fashion enthusiasts with a solid starting point for their education and practice in this field.

Second Part

Advanced Terminology and Technique

Haute Couture: The French high fashion that represents the creation of exclusive, tailor-made pieces with high standards of quality and craftsmanship.

Structured Silhouette: Refers to clothing items with a defined and well-structured shape, often made with stiffer fabrics to maintain the form.

Patternmaking: The art of creating patterns for clothing. This process is fundamental in designing and producing garments and requires precision and technical expertise.

Historical Styles and Movements

Art Deco: A style that developed in the 1920s and 1930s, known for its geometric patterns and symmetrical designs. It influenced fashion in terms of jewelry, clothing, and accessories.

Belle Époque: A historical period characterized by luxurious lifestyles and elaborate fashion, with clothing emphasizing femininity and sophistication.

Dandyism: A fashion style associated with men who dress elegantly and refined, paying great attention to details and the quality of fabrics.

Emerging Trends and Contemporary Terminology

Athleisure: A trend that combines sportswear with casual fashion, resulting in a look that is both functional and stylistically conscious.

Upcycling: The practice of transforming used materials or scraps into new products of higher quality or aesthetic value, often with a focus on sustainability.

Minimalism: A style that focuses on simplicity and functionality, characterized by clean lines, neutral color palettes, and a no-frills design.

Personal Shopping Terminology

Wardrobe Audit: The process of reviewing and evaluating a client's wardrobe, identifying which items to keep, alter, or remove.

Body Type Analysis: The analysis of a client's body proportions and shape to select clothing items that are most flattering and appropriate.

Personal Branding: The process of creating and communicating a unique image or identity for the client through clothing and personal style.

FREQUENTLY ASKED QUESTIONS: WHAT ARE THE MOST IMPORTANT TERMS TO KNOW IN FASHION?

In the world of fashion, some terms are essential for anyone looking to deepen their knowledge or work in the industry. Here's a selection of the most important terms:

1. **Silhouette**: This term describes the basic shape of a clothing item on the body. Understanding different silhouettes, such as A-line, empire, or shift, is essential for choosing clothes that best suit different figures.

2. **Haute Couture**: Refers to exclusive, customized fashion pieces, handcrafted by specialized ateliers. It's an important term to understand high fashion and its impact on trends.

3. **Prêt-à-Porter**: Also known as "ready-to-wear," this term refers to fashion collections produced in bulk, as opposed to custom haute couture.

4. **Draping**: A design technique where fabric is artistically and fluidly arranged around the body, creating elegant lines and shapes.

5. **Minimalism**: A design style that focuses on simplicity and the use of a few essential elements, characterized by clean lines and neutral color palettes.

6. **Upcycling**: The practice of recycling used materials or scraps

into new fashion products, often with a focus on sustainability and innovation.

7. **Vintage**: Refers to fashion items that are at least 20 years old, often sought after for their unique style and craftsmanship.

8. **Fast Fashion**: A term used to describe rapid, low-cost production practices that enable fashion retailers to quickly bring new styles to the market.

These terms represent just some of the fundamental aspects of the fashion language. Understanding them can significantly enrich your knowledge of the industry and enhance your ability to navigate the world of fashion with greater confidence and competence.

DEBUNKING MYTHS: FASHION IS FILLED WITH INCOMPREHENSIBLE TERMS

The world of fashion is often perceived as a labyrinth of technical terms and specialized jargon, which may seem intimidating to those not in the industry. However, the reality is much more accessible and understandable than this myth suggests. Fashion is not an exclusive field for experts or industry professionals; it is a universe that anyone can learn to navigate.

Accessibility of Fashion Language: Many terms used in fashion have entered common language. Words like "vintage," "trendy," or "casual" are used regularly, demonstrating that the language of fashion is not as inaccessible as one might think.

Educational Resources: With an abundance of resources available, from specialized magazines to blogs, online courses, and video tutorials, learning specific fashion terms has become easier than ever.

Intuitive Terminology: Many fashion terms intuitively describe what they represent. For example, "A-line" for a skirt or dress indicates a silhouette that resembles the letter "A," making the understanding of many concepts easier.

Fashion Evolution: The language of fashion is continuously changing, with new terms emerging to describe styles, trends, and technologies. This dynamism makes the industry always exciting, and learning new terms is part of the fun of staying updated.

Pop Culture and Fashion: The representation of fashion and its terms in pop culture, in movies, TV series, and songs, helps make the language of fashion part of common cultural discourse.

Fashion is for Everyone: It is essential to remember that fashion is self-expression and an art accessible to all. You don't need to know every technical term to appreciate or participate in the world of fashion.

In conclusion, despite the fashion industry having its specific jargon, this should not be a barrier for those interested in exploring it. Thanks to curiosity and available resources, fashion terms can be easily learned and understood, making this fascinating and creative world open to everyone.

CONCLUSION

As we approach the conclusion of this journey through the vast and colorful world of fashion and personal shopping, it's time to reflect on what we have explored and learned. We have navigated through the complexities and nuances of fashion, from the crucial role of personal shoppers and image consultants to the rich tapestry of styles, fabrics, and trends that characterize this dynamic industry.

We have discovered how personal image and style can have a profound impact not only on an individual's self-esteem but also on how others perceive them. We have examined how image consultants work meticulously to enhance each individual, demonstrating that the art of personal shopping goes far beyond simply selecting clothes: it is a process of transformation and personal expression.

In the sections dedicated to fabrics, colors, and various clothing styles, we have provided tools and knowledge to help every reader express their individuality through fashion. We have addressed myths and misconceptions, opening the door to a deeper and more inclusive understanding of what fashion can represent for each of us.

This book has been more than just a guide; it has been an invitation to embark on a personal journey into the world of fashion. Each chapter has been a step toward understanding that fashion is not just what we wear but a reflection of who we are, our stories, and our aspirations.

As we close this final chapter, the journey does not end here. Fashion is a constantly evolving world, filled with new trends, challenges, and opportunities. We invite our readers to continue exploring, experimenting, and, above all, enjoying the joy and self-expression that fashion can bring to their lives.

Be bold, be curious, and most importantly, be yourself. This is the true spirit of fashion.

AUTHOR'S NOTE

Gianni Valente is the pseudonym of a prominent figure in the world of fashion and personal shopping, recognized for his deep knowledge and innate ability to transform clothing into an expression of personal identity and style. Born and raised in Italy, a country renowned for its aesthetic sensibilities and design heritage, Gianni developed a passion for fashion and the art of dressing from a young age.

After earning a degree in Fashion Design from one of Italy's most prestigious institutions, Gianni began his career working with various high-end fashion brands. His experiences took him around the world, collaborating with internationally acclaimed designers and gaining a global perspective on the diverse cultures of fashion. These experiences enriched his approach to fashion, allowing him to blend traditional techniques with contemporary trends.

Gianni then specialized as an image consultant and personal shopper, helping clients discover and enhance their personal style. His philosophy is based on the belief that fashion is much more than mere trends; it is a means of expressing individuality and boosting self-confidence.

In addition to his work with private clients, Gianni has conducted courses and seminars on style and personal image, becoming an influential educator in the field. His ability to communicate complex concepts clearly and engagingly has made him a highly sought-after speaker at fashion events and workshops.

The decision to write a book stemmed from Gianni's desire to share his wealth of knowledge with a broader audience. In his book, "Beyond Fashion: The Path to Becoming a Personal Shopper and Image Consultant," Gianni offers not only his extensive experience but also his vision and passion for fashion, making it essential reading for anyone aspiring to understand and master the art of personal shopping and image consultancy.

Gianni Valente continues to be a prominent figure in the industry, constantly inspiring those seeking to find their voice in the vibrant world of fashion.

Discover a World of Knowledge and Inspiration

Visit www.libriutili.it

Dear reader,

We hope you have found inspiration and utility within the pages of this book. If your thirst for knowledge and personal growth is not yet satisfied, we have a special surprise for you!

We invite you to explore the world of LuminaLibria at www.libriutili.it, where a universe of books awaits you. LuminaLibria is an oasis for every type of reader, offering a wide range of genres that will enrich your reading experience.

For Young Explorers: Browse our collection of Children's Books and Stories for Children, perfect for igniting the imagination and curiosity of the youngest readers.

For Art and Relaxation: Let yourself be captivated by our Adult and Children's Coloring Books, a creative way to relax and express yourself.

For Personal Growth: Explore our Self-Help, Personal Growth, and Biographies Books to inspire and motivate you on your life journey.

For the Curious Spirits: Deepen your spiritual path with our Books on Spiritual Themes.

This is only a small part of what LuminaLibria has to offer. We believe that every book is a window to new worlds, ideas, and possibilities. Whether you're seeking adventure, knowledge, or inspiration, you'll find a book that speaks to your heart at www.libriutili.it. And remember, our books are available in English, Italian, and Spanish.

Scan the QR code below to begin your journey into the world of LuminaLibria.

Thank you for joining us on this journey of discovery and growth. We're excited to see you explore even more with LuminaLibria.

Happy reading and continued exploration!

The LuminaLibria Team